Children's Television

Children's
Television

THE ECONOMICS OF EXPLOITATION

William Melody

New Haven and London, Yale University Press

Library of Congress catalog card number: 73-80079
International standard book number: 0-300-01654-9 (cloth),
0-300-01707-3 (paper)

Designed by Sally Sullivan
and set in Baskerville type.
Printed in the United States of America by
The Colonial Press Inc., Clinton, Mass.

Published in Great Britain, Europe, and Africa by
Yale University Press, Ltd., London.
Distributed in Latin America by Kaiman & Polon,
Inc., New York City; in Australasia and Southeast
Asia by John Wiley & Sons Australasia Pty. Ltd.,
Sydney; in India by UBS Publishers' Distributors Pvt.,
Ltd., Delhi; in Japan by John Weatherhill, Inc., Tokyo.

To Children
especially Sue Marie, Sandy, Chrissy, and Jill

Contents

Preface

In recent years the focusing of public attention on children's television has been due, in substantial part, to the activities of Action for Children's Television (ACT). ACT was spawned by the concern of some observant mothers about the characteristics of commercial television programming and advertising directed at children and the potential consequences for, and effects on, children. In like manner, the author's interest in the economic and public-policy aspects of commercial children's television has been stimulated significantly by the efforts of ACT. Peggy Charren, president, and Evelyn Sarson, executive director of ACT, have been articulate advocates before regulatory agencies, Congress, and other interested groups for special consideration of the interests of children in the policies of commercial television program managers, advertisers, and regulators.

They also challenged the author to study the economic characteristics of commercial children's television, to examine its economic forces and trends, and to evaluate the alternative directions that public policy toward commercial children's television by the Federal Communications Commission (FCC) might take. This study attests to the fact that such a challenge could not, and cannot, be dismissed lightly. ACT has forced us all to ask some very fundamental questions about the roles that television programming and advertising directed at children do play, and should play, in the lives of our children. It was my inability to provide satisfactory answers to many of their questions that ultimately led to the present study.

The original study was prepared under a grant from the John and Mary R. Markle Foundation to the University of Pennsylvania. That study was submitted to the FCC in January 1973 as part of testimony before the Commission at its hearings on children's television. The present study represents a revision and updating of the original study in light of the FCC hearings and other more recent developments that affect the children's television issues.

In the course of research for this study, many people from the industrial, governmental, and university communities, as well as independent experts and scholars, were contacted for information and discussion on various questions relating to the economic and public-policy aspects of children's television. Most were extremely helpful and cooperative. Although they cannot be acknowledged individually here, at least their collective assistance should be recognized. Particular acknowledgment is due to Robert Lewis Shayon, a colleague at the University of Pennsylvania, who has carried an abiding interest in children's television for many years, and who, more than twenty years ago, in his book, *Television and Our Children* (New York: Longmans, Green, 1951) pointed to many of the current issues in children's television. Also Alan Pearce of the FCC, author of "The Economics of Network Children's Television Programming" (FCC, 1972), was most helpful in discussing his study as well as other aspects of the economics of commercial children's television.

Most important, I must acknowledge the substantial contribution of my research assistants, Wendy Ehrlich and Douglas Richardson. At the time of the study, they were graduate students at The Annenberg School of Communications, University of Pennsylvania. They devoted the summer of 1972 to research on children's television, they actively participated in the development of the study, and they have performed beyond the call of duty throughout its preparation. Panthea Wilson typed several manuscript drafts with her usual degree of outstanding competence, efficiency, and good humor. My wife Jill provided patience, understanding, and periodic pungent observation, including an occasional request that I stop studying about "children" so that I could spend some time with my own. Finally, I must thank my children for making me watch so much children's television, thereby providing continuous positive reinforcement to the challenge of ACT.

W. H. M.

Philadelphia, Pennsylvania
April 1973

1. Introduction

There are high public interest considerations involved in the use of television. . . . in relation to a large and important segment of the audience, the Nation's children. The importance of this portion of the audience, and the character of material reaching it, are particularly great because its ideas and concepts are largely not yet crystallized and are therefore open to suggestion, and also because its members do not yet have the experience and judgment always to distinguish the real from the fanciful.[1]

So observed the Federal Communications Commission (FCC) in its Notice of Inquiry into children's television in January 1971. The notice provided formal recognition of a petition to the Commission by Action for Children's Television (ACT) to the effect that most commercial television programming and advertising directed at children is not in their interest and, in fact, is actually harmful to them in many ways. With its notice, the FCC brought the ACT petition into the arena of public-policy debate by taking the first legal step in the deliberative process that could lead to the formulation of public policy in the field of commercial children's television.

Society has always considered the world of children to be something unique, requiring that special responsibilities be assumed by adults in many of their relations with children. Poets and philosophers, statesmen and politi-

1

cians, businessmen and public-policy-makers, judges and parents have all spoken eloquently of the very specialized character of children and of society's responsibility to set them apart from the general rules of acceptable adult behavior.

The responsibilities of society toward children are of two kinds. First, we have special protections designed to shield children from predatory adult exploitation and to insulate them from certain responsibilities in their dealings with adults. For example, children may not be made legally responsible for contracts, they may not purchase alcoholic beverages, and they are protected from employment abuses by child labor laws. Such precautions are intended to prevent exploitation by adults of the particular vulnerability of children.

Second, there are specific responsibilities for providing special services to children that will facilitate their constructive growth and maturation. Most of these responsibilities can be classified under a broad interpretation of education. Society recognizes that its most precious resource is its children and that it thus has a responsibility to provide a positive program of enrichment to meet their particular needs and interests.

However, this does not mean that children are singled out for specialized treatment in every aspect of their lives. Nor are they isolated from all of life's more sordid aspects. Children are exposed to the adult world and at least observe many of its exploitative characteristics. Indeed, some exposure is necessary as part of the instructional and educational processes. Children are not protected from responsibility in all of their dealings with adults, nor should they be.

Too, adult society does not assume total responsibility for their education, enrichment, and maturing to adulthood. Society provides only selected protections for children and assumes only certain responsibilities to them. These change over time, as the methods and technology for exploiting and educating children and the values of society change. But generally the concern of society has been directed toward the protection of children from specific and direct exploitation by adults, and toward the enrichment of children by means of specific and direct responses to their particular needs and interests. The public policy issue today is whether commercial children's television is an area that requires the establishment of special protections for children and/or positive responsibilities to them.

CHILDREN AND COMMERCIAL TELEVISION

Over the past quarter-century, the relatively new technology of television has grown to be an enormously effective tool for commercial marketing in the United States. Television has become the most dominant medium for advertising, and present trends indicate that in the future television will play an even more important role as an advertising and marketing device.

In recent years, public concern over the consequences of commercial television practices that are directed at lucrative children's markets has continued to mount. This public reaction has reflected concern both for the protection of children from direct, pinpoint exploitation via seductive and misleading advertising, and for the responsibilities of commercial broadcast stations. They are licensed as "public trustees" charged with special responsibilities to serve the public interest, and to develop television programming specifically designed to meet the needs and interests of children rather than those of merchants who sell to, and through, children. In January 1971, when the FCC published its Notice of Inquiry on children's television, it requested comments from interested parties on a proposal by ACT to remove commercials from children's television and to require a minimum quantity of age-specific programming produced to meet the interests of children. Thus, the issue of specialized treatment for children by commercial television broadcasters was clearly drawn. Should special protections be provided to insulate children from direct advertising designed to stimulate their consumption desires so that they would become active lobbyists for the merchandiser within the family? Should public policy recognize a responsibility to provide a minimal level of programming on commercial stations specifically directed to the needs and interests of children? These questions, in turn, raise the broader issue posed by FCC chairman Burch as to "whether a commercially-based broadcasting system is capable of serving up quality programming for an audience so sensitive and malleable as children.[2]

ECONOMIC CONSEQUENCES OF INSTITUTIONAL CHANGE

It is inevitable that changes in public policy will have economic consequences for the various institutions that perform certain functions in the television industry and have acquired vested interests in the existing structure of the industry. It is also inevitable that those institutions that do not stand to gain from a proposed policy change will predict dire economic consequences if any change is made. Potential economic consequences are advanced by vested interests as providing such an overwhelming constraint that otherwise worthy objectives are rendered infeasible, and therefore cannot even be seriously considered. In the face of such opposition, the task of differentiating probable from alarmist predictions of economic consequences becomes quite formidable, as does the task of designing feasible plans for change that could accommodate the necessary economic limitations.

In the area of children's television, the most significant objections to proposals such as that filed with the FCC by ACT are economic issues. On the one hand, it is claimed that the loss of advertising revenues from children's television by broadcast stations and networks might create a severe financial hardship for those firms. On the other hand, alternative sources of financing may not be forthcoming to ensure that children's programming is provided on commercial broadcasting at all. If these fears are accepted automatically as constraints, can the FCC seriously consider attempting to implement a plan such as the ACT proposal, no matter how worthy it may appear on other grounds? This study specifically addresses itself to the economic aspects of the issue of commercial children's television and their relation to FCC's public-policy options.

The study addresses three principal questions. First, are the programming and advertising practices in commercial children's television fully explicable in terms of the economic characteristics and market developments in the industry? Is the children's television "problem" an aberration from the normal or expected trend of market development in the industry, or is it part of that trend? Second, does a projection of the trend of economic and market development in the industry indicate that the children's programming and advertising practices that prompted the ACT filing with FCC, and expressions of concern by many other public interest groups, will change for the better or worse? Is market development such that the commercial television market will ultimately prove to be self-correcting and eliminate, or at least reduce, the intensity of these undesirable practices? Or will normal development lead to their expansion and intensification?

Third, in light of the analyses of the first two questions, the study addresses the ACT proposal and the basic economic arguments against its adoption. Is it possible to eliminate advertising from children's television on commercial broadcasting without seriously impairing the broadcast industries financially? If advertising is eliminated from commercial children's television, is alternative financing likely to be forthcoming, or will children's programming disappear? Is it possible to develop a program for change without requiring unacceptable risks that such a program will not be achieved and that, instead, the only result will be that detrimental consequences will be borne by established industrial institutions?

After examining these questions, the study concludes with the presentation of a plan by which the FCC could implement the ACT proposal without significant financial hardship to established industry institutions and with minimum risk of unacceptable public consequences.

OUTLINE OF THE STUDY

This study deals with the economics of children's television within the institutional structure of the broadcasting industry, the framework for developing public policy in commercial broadcasting, and the fundamental economic forces affecting the direction of development of the industry. Chapter 2 delineates the basic economic model of commercial broadcasting, emphasizing the unique methods broadcasters use to sell audiences to advertisers under a system where programs serve primarily as bait to attract the viewers. The primary industrial institutions, their economic roles within the industry, and their interrelationships are discussed.

The history of children's television is analyzed in chapter 3. It emphasizes the apparent economic incentives for the development of children's television along certain lines and the conflicts between commercial interests and children's interests in determining the kinds, quantities, and hours of children's television. In particular, contrasts are drawn among the treatment of children's television during the promotional era of television, the mass-marketing era, and the more recent era of marketing specialized children's audiences to advertisers.

The unique economic characteristics of children's television are developed in chapter 4. It is demonstrated that the classification of children by broadcasters as a specialized audience, although based upon the particular viewing habits, sensibilities, and perceptions of children, is made almost entirely for purposes of attracting particular child audiences that can be effectively sold to advertisers. However, the potential of the child audience as a specialized market for advertisers need have no relationship to those attributes which would govern the classifications of specialized child audiences if programming is to be responsive to the needs and interests of children.

Perhaps the great irony of the children's television issue is that complaints from the public about the need for age-specific and other kinds of specialized children's television have surfaced with intensity at precisely the time when the broadcast industry has begun to increase specialization in children's programming, including age-specific programming. In fact, it is precisely the industry practices relating to specialization in children's audiences as a means for isolating specialized advertiser markets that have stimulated the complaints about advertiser abuses. It is to these audiences that the direct, pinpoint application of the latest persuasive advertising techniques on the child viewer have been applied. Hence, the real issue is not that of recognizing child audiences as specialized audiences. Rather, the issue is one of the purpose and criteria for specialization. Specialization for pinpoint commercial exploitation is quite different from specialization based upon an objective of enriching particular groups of child viewers.

The development of children's television into a major issue of public policy is examined in chapter 5. The ACT petition to FCC, the FCC Notice of Inquiry and Proposed Rulemaking, and the response of the broadcasting industry, are reviewed and analyzed. The study on "The Economics of Network Children's Television," undertaken by Alan Pearce for the FCC, is critically examined as a benchmark for FCC policy-making in children's television.

Chapter 6 recognizes that, although the problems of children's television have been recognized by the FCC as matters for policy consideration, there are inevitable questions that must be raised relating to the specific responsibilities of the Commission, the limits of its legal authority, and the range of alternative policy options that it could adopt. This chapter reviews and assesses the role of FCC regulation as it could be brought to bear on the children's television issues raised in the ACT proposal.

Chapter 7 addresses the fundamental issue of whether the objectives of protecting children from being selected for pinpoint advertiser exploitation and ensuring that they are singled out for special programming on the basis of their own needs and interests can be met within the existing framework of our commercial broadcast system. A forecast of industry developments under existing arrangements indicates that the trend toward market specialization in children's television will not only continue but intensify. Audience markets will tend to become tailored more closely to advertiser requirements, and the programs and advertisements will be made more effective in exploiting the vulnerabilities of children. Thus, the harmful effects that many people already see existing in children's television are much more likely to increase than to decrease. The problem is not one that shows any signs of correcting itself.

Moreover, the trend toward profitable market segmentation of children's television is not likely to be modified by good intentions or self-regulation. Over time, the financial sacrifice of failing to develop specialized children's markets for advertisers will be continuously increasing. The profits that would be foregone from not exploiting the child markets make it virtually inevitable that the broadcasters will pursue a path of more intensive development of specialized child audiences as markets to be sold to advertisers. It appears inevitable that the presently operative economic forces in the industry will work to make the problems that prompted the ACT proposal more serious. Yet, the increased profitability from children's television and the expansion and extension of vested interests in television advertising to children will make it even more difficult for public-policy-makers to come to grips with the problem in the future.

Of the range of public-policy options, external financing is the only alternative not requiring the FCC to get the broadcast industry to modify its fundamental profit-making and market-protection objectives internally. However, the corollary problems of financing pose serious issues of the cost and risk involved in such a major structural adjustment. Yet, when one recognizes that institutional change does not have to take place instantaneously, with cataclysmic economic consequences, it becomes clear that policy-makers could phase in the new policy at whatever rate they find most compatible with the public interest. Thus, whatever economic constraints exist, they become factors that preclude neither the feasibility of change nor the direction of change.

A point-of-reference plan is outlined as an example of a manageable and reasonable transitional program for implementing the ACT proposal. A planning horizon of five to seven years might be adopted for phasing out advertiser support of children's television and phasing in alternative methods of financing. As the first step in a several-step transition procedure, one hour per week of programming by each network for a national audience, and one hour per week of programming by local stations, could be adopted. Expansion of children's programming under the new arrangements could proceed under FCC guidance as circumstances permit. Year-to-year assessments of the financial impact upon the broadcast industry and the rate of development of alternative sources of program financing might provide a basis for an orderly changeover, without requiring that significant risks be assumed by any segment of the industry. The point-of-reference plan is intended to provide a foundation for the development of an actual plan by the FCC, based upon its examination and analysis of more detailed industry data, for implementation as policy.

2. Institutions and Markets in Television Broadcasting

Although children's television represents only one small segment of the total program output of the broadcasting industry, its production, distribution, and broadcast characteristics are influenced significantly by the same basic industrial and market forces that determine the supply of all kinds of programs. Thus, any evaluation of the consequences of proposed changes in children's television must recognize the possible effects upon existing institutions and market relationships in the television industry as a whole. This chapter outlines the dominant institutions and market relationships in broadcasting, and provides the necessary background for evaluating specific proposals relating to children's television.

THE BASIC MODEL OF COMMERCIAL BROADCASTING

As in most industries, the institutions in broadcasting do not all perform singular and clear-cut functions. Firms in the commercial television industries often simultaneously perform several industrial functions and shift their activities over time. In order to distill the essential economic characteristics of commercial broadcasting, one must examine the functions that are being performed and/or the primary institutions performing them. First, let us examine the basic industry functions and their market interrelationships.

In economic terms, goods and services are exchanged

11

in markets, the market being the place where buyers and sellers of particular products and services are brought together for the purpose of transacting exchanges. The exchange of goods and services in markets results from the operation of an interactive process that brings together potential buyers with particular product or service demands, and potential sellers who design their products or services to meet the particular demands of potential buyers.

Traditional conceptions of the operations of broadcast systems presume that the potential viewing audiences represent the demands to which the system tries to respond, i.e. programs are designed, produced, and broadcast in response to direct assessments of the needs and desires of the viewing audiences. However, in a commercial broadcast system, the paying customer to whom the market responds is not the viewing audience but, rather, the advertiser. In turn, the viewing audience is not the customer in the market but, rather, the product being sold. The advertiser is buying an audience, and the bait for attracting an audience is a program.

Of course, this does not mean that the interests of advertisers and viewing audiences are diametrically opposed. In many respects their interests overlap and lie in the same direction. Yet, it is most important to recognize that the system is fundamentally responsive to the advertiser. The interests of viewing audiences are satisfied only when they happen to correspond with the interests of advertisers. In short, the operation of all aspects of the broadcast system is uniquely conditioned to the needs and requirements of advertisers. As Figure 1 illustrates, the television program is merely the vehicle for bringing together the advertiser and the audience.

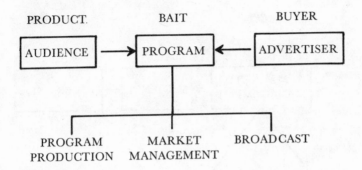

Figure 1. Operation of the Commercial Broadcast System

Bringing the advertiser and the audience together is a task that involves the performance of essentially three basic functions: (1) the production of programs; (2) the marketing of audiences, i.e. bringing audience and advertiser together through the lure of programs and consummating sale; and (3) the broadcasting of programs and advertisements to audiences. The broadcasting networks are the primary market managers for national programs, while the stations perform a similar function for local programs. The market managers acquire programs, establish networks of broadcasting stations which determine the size and characteristics of the potential audiences for programs, and sell the program-audience package to advertisers.

The fundamental economic exchange in broadcast markets takes place between the market-manager (network or station) and the advertiser. As Figure 2 illustrates, the market manager brings to the market a product package that will permit an advertiser to reach a particular audience, e.g. a mass viewing audience of a potential numerical size, or a specialized audience such

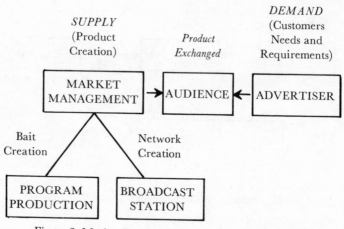

Figure 2. Market Exchange in Commercial Broadcasting

as housewives, sports fans, or children. The package consists of programs designed to attract this particular kind of audience and a willingness to sell advertising time on broadcast stations or networks. The product exchanged between the market manager and the advertiser is access to a wide variety of audiences.

The price of the audience "product" depends upon the size, demographic, and other market characteristics of the audience, as well as the day and hour of broadcast. Hence, the audiences being sold can be highly differentiated according to the marketing criteria for advertising particular kinds of products. Program creation and production is directed toward attracting audiences of particular sizes and compositions that will be increasingly valuable and saleable to advertisers. Economic success is achieved when audiences that will be responsive to the advertiser's objective of convincing them to buy his product can be delivered. The more effective the advertising is with a particular audience, the higher the rates for advertising to that audience, and the higher the profits for the television industry.

The types of programs that will be broadcast at any particular time depend significantly upon the alternative uses to which that time period could be put, i.e. the alternative audiences and advertisers that would be attracted, and the profits that would be realized, if different programs were employed. Therefore, programs that are actually broadcast are not based upon absolute measures of their "audience," but on relative measures of audience in comparison with the other possible audiences that could be created at the same time. Most programs would attract their greatest audiences during prime time. But shows that would rank second-best in advertiser attractiveness and profitability during prime-time hours, and at other hours as well, will likely never be produced or shown, no matter how large their absolute audience would be at any particular time.

Thus, children's television is broadcast not when it is most convenient for children, or when the largest children's audiences would be attracted, but rather when children's television provides the greatest commercial advantage over alternative programming at that particular time. The largest number of child viewers are available in the late afternoon hours after school. But except for some UHF stations, this time period can be more profitably devoted to other kinds of programming, e.g. for the housewife market. On weekend mornings, fewer child viewers may be watching, but children's programming is by far the most profitable alternative.

Viewer program choices in broadcasting are severely limited because the market from which programs can be selected is not competitive in the true economic sense. Although the viewer has a choice of more than one program, his choices are limited by the number of operating channels and the programming that happens to be provided on them at any particular time. But most important is the fact that competitive entry into most broadcast markets that would increase viewer choice and could stimulate the responsiveness of existing broadcasters to viewer interests is virtually closed. The licensing of broadcast stations is highly regulated by governmental authority because freedom of entry into competitive markets is not possible in broadcasting. Thus, in commercial broadcasting, government regulation replaces the force of free market competition in attempting to get broadcasters to respond to the needs and interests of the public it serves.

In attracting audiences, market managers may seek the largest mass audience possible, i.e. the greatest number of eyeballs, or they may seek a smaller, specialized audience that is likely to be more receptive to the messages of particular types of advertisers. From the mass audience, an advertiser expects his expenditure to produce only a relatively small proportionate response from a large audience. From the specialized audience, an advertiser expects a relatively larger proportionate response from a smaller audience. Most of children's television is illustrative of specialized programming for specialized audiences and specialized advertisers.

Other significant variables in programming decisions are the number and kind of competitive programs and programming costs. If competitors are few, it is frequently more profitable to aim for a proportionate share of a mass audience. If competitors are many, there is more incentive to consider seeking a specialized audience. Also, when mass audiences would be large, it is generally in the economic interest of market-managers and advertisers to seek a share of the mass audience. When mass audiences would be small, the alternative of specialization is frequently more profitable. Further, differences in program costs and quality may or may not influence the size and structure of an audience. Some specialized audiences, such as the weekend morning "children's television ghetto," which may not change significantly in size regardless of the quality of programming, can be served more profitably at minimum levels of program cost. For other audiences, programming of higher cost and quality may be necessary to maintain the audience.

BROADCASTING INSTITUTIONS

Having reviewed the basic functions in commercial broadcasting, we now direct our attention to the primary institutions that perform these functions. Their economic roles within the industry and their relationships with other major institutions will be examined briefly.

Advertisers

Advertisers buy time on local stations and national networks to present advertising messages to particular audiences. Broadcast advertising may be purchased in units of varying length from these sources. When an advertiser buys "program time" in units of five minutes or more, he is considered a "sponsor" of that program. In most instances, however, the advertiser buys "spot announcement time" in units of two minutes or less, suitable just for the presentation of a commercial message. There are national advertisers who market their products on a national or regional scale, and local advertisers who basically only serve a single community. Together, they are the paying customers to whom the broadcasting industry must respond if it is to achieve financial success. In 1971, advertisers spent \$3.2 billion on television.[1]

Having selected the type of audience he desires, the advertiser tends to equate greater exposure with greater sales. In seeking the greatest exposure to potential buyers of his products or services, the advertiser allocates a budget—usually based upon the previous year's allocations and performance—and hires one or more advertising agencies. Advertisers with sophisticated internal market analysis divisions may allocate their budgets among all advertising media—e.g. television, radio, newspapers, magazines, etc.—for maximum efficiency, and then hire agencies on the basis of particular skill in a given medium.

Agencies customarily earn a 15 percent commission on the total advertising dollars they place.[2] Agency turnover is common, and the advertiser generally maintains substantial control over the advertising program. Although the agency is specialized to plan strategy, determine markets, plot campaigns, produce commercials, and buy time for ad placement, the specialized mechanisms of the agency are most frequently tailored to reinforce advertiser directives.

For purposes of examining broadcast institutions, however, the advertiser and his agency can be viewed as a single market force. Acting in concert, they are responsible for the decisions to buy airtime from networks and stations. They are responsible for the production of advertisements, either directly or under contract to production houses. They are responsible for the emphasis presently put on audience ratings as an index of audience response and therefore of advertising efficiency. A ratio of the cost per thousand viewers in audiences of different sizes usually determines the effectiveness of advertising budget allocations. Programs attracting a large proportion of the audience the advertiser is interested in reaching, at a lower cost per thousand than is available at other times, are usually considered to be an efficient allocation of advertising expenditures.

For many products sheer numbers of viewers are relatively less significant than the constitution of the audiences. Because advertisers want to reach specific groups—e.g. housewives, rural people, teenagers, children, or those over fifty—a strategy of time-buying has evolved, in which advertisers can place ads in certain markets at certain times that best meet their specific advertising needs. The agency representing a local advertiser will buy broadcast time directly from the local television station for penetration of a single, local market. Agencies representing national or regional advertisers may purchase time from a network for national audiences, or they may deal with the station representative agencies, which work on behalf of the stations that commission them to sell their own available advertising time ("national spot" advertising). In addition, station representatives assist stations in determining appropriate rates for airtime, in developing sales promotional materials, and in planning trade advertising for the station. Station representatives also earn a 15 percent commission of amounts paid by national advertisers for time on the stations they represent.

Participating sponsorship or spot-announcement buying is claimed to be a higher-efficiency, lower-risk method of allocating an advertising budget than is single or dual sponsorship, in which one or two advertisers assume the entire cost of presenting a program or a program series, i.e. pay production costs and network or station time costs for showing the program. In this way, the advertiser can spread his message in order to get the greatest possible market penetration among the audiences he desires and is not locked into a single time-period. He faces less risk and incurs lower costs. Formerly, if "his" program was a failure, the advertiser faced losses, both because a program he had paid for had failed and because the program had served as an inefficient vehicle for advertising. Whether sponsoring or participating, however, advertisers have a significant voice in the types of programs the networks and stations broadcast. Although the networks and stations generally select or produce the programs themselves, the epitaph of "no sponsor interest" has killed many a potential program.

The development of participation and of specialized market penetration has meant the rapid development of national spot selling; in 1970, about 22 percent of advertising sales were local, 30 percent were placed on the networks, and 48 percent went to national spot advertising.[3] It is noteworthy that the specialization of the agency function has continued apace, even giving rise to new sub-institutions. Many agencies, for example, are now relying heavily on computers to digest a vast amount of marketing information, ratings values, and information on available resources to develop a full-blown placement and marketing strategy. Moreover, the complexity of placing spots in many markets at many times has become so great that firms that do nothing but buy time on behalf of agencies have begun to flourish. It is even possible to subscribe to electronic monitoring services, which are continually being improved. In many markets, then, we have a multitiered institutional operation: time-buyers and monitoring services; market research firms; commercial production arms; strategy planners and operations specialists—all under the aegis of the advertising agency, which is, in turn, the agent of the advertiser.

Acting together, these institutions exert enormous pressure on the form that present television assumes; those responsible for planning and producing programming cannot work autonomously from those who ultimately supply the resources for this activity. The goals of the advertiser, therefore, whether or not they coincide with those of other institutions or with the interests of the public, are bound to find substantial expression in what eventually is broadcast. And as the advertising function becomes more and more specialized and specifically responsive to audiences of potential buyers, the broadcasting structure can be expected to become more responsive to the needs of advertisers for effective product marketing.

Program Producers

Examination of the characteristics of program production reveals many of the same economic factors that governed the behavior of advertisers and agencies. Once again there has been institutional response to the problems of allocating resources, assuming risk, integrating immediate goals with the larger imperatives of the system, maintaining revenues, and producing a product in an environment where diverse forces are at work.

The networks themselves do some of their own production, primarily in the areas of news, live special events, sports events, talk shows, and some live entertainment programming. They also rent their facilities and talent to

other producers. Local stations do some program production for their own, and perhaps other, stations' use—
and, in fact, they are required by the FCC to do some
program production. The true "production houses,"
however, are the independent or subsidiary companies of
larger firms. Many of the major motion-picture companies have established television production subdivisions,
such as MCA Inc. (Universal Pictures), Screen Gems
(Columbia Pictures), and Warner Brothers Television
(Warner Communications). The truly independent production houses generally work on a one-shot basis, the
more successful ones with a long-running network or
syndicated series that sustains them.

A number of other institutions engage in program
production for use on commercial television in varying
degrees, such as the advertisers and their agencies and
various government agencies. According to a recent
report,[4] the U.S. government now ranks as the nation's
single largest producer of television, radio, motion-picture and other audiovisual material.

Production as a process, however, reveals its fundamental economic characteristics only when the operation
of production is integrated with the forces surrounding
the development of programming. It is in program
development that the industry relationships constrain
and direct the economic activity of producers and
thereby directly influence the nature of the programs
produced. Program development "is distantly related to
what large industries call research and development, the
continuing investment of money and manpower in
exploration of new products for the future."[5]

In broadcasting, that activity revolves around "pilot"-
making—a preview film that gives both an indication of
how the idea will bear translation to production and how

competently the production house can fashion that translation. Even if a program developed in this manner is rejected, often thousands of dollars have already been invested in it. Thus deficit financing is unavoidable with mass program development and pilot-making activities— a risk few producers can, or are willing to assume on their own. Most often, outside financing is employed, either from the potential buyer of the program, or from other sources.

The primary potential buyers for new program production are the networks, which have acquired a high degree of control over program production. A structural reason for the concentration of control over program development with the networks, of great concern to the FCC, is the claim over station schedules by the networks, leaving affiliated stations little desirable time to fill with non-network programming. For this reason, in an attempt to break the grip of monopoly power by the networks over prime-time programming, the FCC issued its Prime Time Access rule in 1970, limiting commercial stations in the top fifty broadcast markets to no more than three hours of network programs during the prime evening hours. This rule is intended to open prime-time programming to some degree of competition from alternative program sources. More recently, the Antitrust Division of the Department of Justice charged the networks with violation of the antitrust laws in their monopolization of prime-time programming.

Because the product exchanged between the networks and advertisers involves a "package" consisting of programs and access to audiences, it is of paramount importance to the networks to continue to provide a product that will meet the needs of advertisers. The level of network interaction with production firms thus often begins before an idea for the program is even conceived. Sometimes the network will create an idea and seek out a studio to develop it. Or the studio may create or buy an idea and sell it to the network for development into a series. But no matter where the ideas come from, the network must approve them or the show is not likely to get on the air.[6] In return, the network assumes most of the financial risk involved in development and production, determining, in effect, how large a profit the producer will be allowed to enjoy. If not technically a cost-plus operation, it is indeed a symbiotic relationship.

It is in this market environment that production houses must compete with one another. For large houses, continuity—the knowledge that networks will keep returning to them for new series, specials, or movies—has become all important. Just as network decisions concerning program content are circumscribed by advertiser demands, so the production house surrenders much of its creative autonomy in exchange for relative market security. Being an "in" producer guarantees a stable and continuing source of revenue. Being an "out" producer means that there is no access to the primary market in which the product can be sold.

The management philosophy of the networks toward program production was perhaps best described by CBS in its 1963 Annual Report to Stockholders:

> The ability to produce a program schedule which year after year commands the largest audiences in broadcasting is founded on a steadfast commitment to two fundamental programming principles. The first is to obtain the talents of those writers, producers, directors and performers whose outstanding abilities and dedication permit no compromise with anything less than

their best efforts at all times. The second is the continuing participation of the Network's programming officials at every stage of the creative process from the initial script to the final broadcast. This applies not only to the occasional special program, but to the day-to-day production of continuing program series.

For the most part, the networks assume the risks, finance program development, assign production to select production houses, decide what ideas will be developed, what programs will be purchased, and what prices will be paid for them.[7]

It is apparent that, generally, program production is carried out by institutions relatively devoid of economic bargaining power. The choice most production houses face is either to produce according to formulae that they do not themselves prescribe, or leave the market. The financing of program development and the control of program access to broadcast stations are such that, although producers may appear to be autonomous business institutions, their fortunes are tied primarily to the decision-making processes of the networks.

Networks

In addition to the functions of planning program development and organizing a program schedule, the national television networks act in five other significant areas: (1) they manage the market for programming on a regular basis; (2) they promote these programs and the network image to the public in order to increase the ratings for network programs; (3) they sell broadcast time to advertisers; (4) they arrange for transmission of these network program/advertising "packages" to the affiliated stations over leased telecommunications facilities; and (5) they oversee the operation of several television stations themselves; the so-called owned and operated (O&O) stations.

It should be noted that, except in their capacity as station owners, the networks are *not* broadcasters, and consequently are not directly regulated by the FCC. However, because the stations owned by the networks are some of the largest and most profitable in the country, policy affecting O&O stations will directly affect network policy.

Since the networks maintain a sales force to solicit advertising in their network schedules, as well as one that sells time for national spot advertising on their O&O stations, the network corporations in effect compete with themselves for proportionate shares of national television advertising expenditures. Of the approximately $1.6 billion expended for television advertising in 1971, 79 percent went to network programming and 15 percent was allocated to the fifteen O&O stations for national spot advertising.

As part of its market management function, the network seeks to ensure that each affiliate carries as large a percentage of network fare as possible. Since network "option clauses" and other restrictive measures were banned by the FCC, each station has the right to clear or not to clear, i.e. show or not show, each network offering. If local needs or financial considerations make it desirable, an individual station should be able to pre-empt or delay (relocate) network fare and substitute syndicated or local programming in its place. This is generally undesirable from the point of view of the networks, however, whose advertising rates are based on their ability to promise audiences of a certain size to the advertiser. If a number of stations choose not to clear an offering, the network must charge lower rates to advertisers.

Therefore, there is considerable pressure on stations to clear network programming. If too many stations refuse to clear the program, the program itself will probably be cancelled; these decisions are generally based upon the audience ratings and advertiser interest. On the other hand, if it appears that a local station is trying to have its cake and eat it too by juggling the network schedule too frequently, it may be faced with the threat of having its network affiliation revoked. Since independent (non-network) stations are seldom as profitable as network affiliates, affiliation is highly valued by stations. One rule of thumb is that affiliates are generally about eight times more profitable than independents. Most affiliates clear a very high percentage—90 percent or more—of the programs offered by their networks.

The networks are able to distribute programs simultaneously to all their affiliates through a special service arrangement with the American Telephone and Telegraph Company (AT&T) whereby AT&T provides transmission channels interconnecting the network "feed" centers to stations all over the country. The rates charged by AT&T for this service are heavily weighted with considerations of continuity and frequency of use. An independent program supplier or "mini-network" such as the regional or special networks for sports, etc. must pay substantially higher prices per hour for their use of these AT&T facilities because of the occasional nature of their use. This rate differential serves effectively to reinforce the market position of the existing networks, and to make entry into the network market prohibitively costly.

The various functions of the networks are coordinated at a central network office in New York. All three networks have now become conglomerate businesses, with the requisite managerial framework necessary for monitoring and evaluating performance in a number of different spheres of activity. Thus, the need exists for extensive planning of future activity and for reducing risk to a minimum. These two goals are both served by the existing industrial structure, in which networks have extensive influence over the activities of most other institutions operating in the television industry.

Program Packagers and Syndicators

An alternative outlet for first-run program production is syndication, but it is a very limited market. As national clearing-houses for new program financing, station clearances and advertising, the networks are formidable competitors for the distributor (known as "program packagers") who operates on a station-by-station basis. For the networks, the costs of administering the facilities necessary to sell (clear) programs to local stations can be recovered over a complete line-up of programs as a continuing operation. Similarly, the unit costs of distributing these programs through a live, interconnected network of stations linked up by transmission lines leased from AT&T are reduced both by the continuous nature of their use and the discriminatory rates in AT&T's tariff.

In syndication, each station taking the syndicated program must be provided with a film print or tape, with its attendant costs and administrative problems. Advertisers prefer to have their commercials centrally integrated into the program, making for much easier monitoring. Unless the advertiser is specifically interested in a spot-sales strategy, station-by-station selling is more costly administratively, and often on a cost per thousand basis as well.

Nevertheless, syndication is an integral part of the broadcasting industry, functioning as a "used program" market for off-network reruns. The revenue-producing life of a network series, if at all successful, seldom ends once the program leaves the network. The domestic and foreign syndication markets keep them in circulation for many years.

Another type of syndicated programming is the resale of theatrical motion pictures for use on television. For a while the networks refused to schedule movies in prime time, but now almost every motion picture made is budgeted with potential television resale value in mind— first to the networks, perhaps, then in syndication to stations.

Television Stations

No two television stations operate exactly alike, and because of this diversity it is often dangerous to generalize about the "average" station. Hence, generalizations must be limited and made with caution. Stations can be categorized, however, by several structural and operational characteristics, such as channel (spectrum space occupied), i.e. VHF (channels 2-12) or UHF (channels 13-80); transmission power; network affiliation status (primary affiliate, secondary affiliate, independent); ownership (part of a broadcast "group" comprised of a number of stations licensed to a common owner, etc.); and market size (the population and income of the community and surrounding area served by the station).

In sum, the range of station activity is diverse, and stations operating under these varying conditions may have quite different economic characteristics.

All commercial broadcast stations are regulated by the federal government. They are licensed by the FCC for a period of three years; at the end of that period the license renewal application is examined to see if that station has been programming in the public interest, as required by federal law. Considerable controversy ranges about the degree of activity necessary for a station to meet its public service obligations, but stations nevertheless feel a continual need to balance profit-making activity with public service activity that will support the broadcaster at license renewal time. At that time, the FCC evaluates the station's performance in terms of responsiveness to local needs and issues, news, religious programming, children's programming, political coverage, and a number of other general public-interest guidelines that have evolved over the years.

As a business operation, however, all commercial stations seek advertising support for the programs they put on the air. These might be programs produced locally by the station's own staff (generally low-budget "service" shows such as news, religion, public affairs). Or they might be programs that have been bought (actually rented) from a syndicator and broadcast by the station. As mentioned in the previous section, these might be first-run programs produced specifically for syndication, but the great majority are off-network programs or theatrical movies that have been released for television. For most network affiliated stations, the great majority of their programming comes from the networks. Stations are paid "compensation" by the networks for the network programs they air, as payment for station airtime and their role in providing additional audiences for the national advertisers who have bought time in these network programs. The amount paid a station as "compensation" is based on a formula accounting for the station's contribution to the national audience for the program, the rate paid the network by the advertisers, and a deduction for production, transmission, and other costs. Thus, although the rate stations are paid for the time they give up to the networks is considerably less than their national spot rates, affiliation assures larger audiences, thus enabling the station to charge higher rates for its own local and national spot advertising that it is allowed to sell during the "station breaks" between and during network programs.

In general, the station serves as the final launching point for programming decisions made further up the line. This does not mean, however, that stations have no influence over the form programming takes. As was noted above, the reluctance to clear a program may bear heavily on that program's fate. Complaints from local audiences may be transmitted back upstream to the networks. The station, too, is faced with the job of balancing forces and economic interests not necessarily coincident with those of the institutions with which it relates. While economic considerations would seem to make the station a relatively weak partner in terms of influencing overall policy decision, it nevertheless acts as a source of peripheral feedback that networks cannot entirely ignore if their strong economic position is to be maintained.

This chapter has focused primarily on the interrelationships between the advertiser/agency, production house, syndicator, network, and station. A number of

institutions have been mentioned which play parts in the
industrial process of broadcasting: for example, the time
sellers, the ratings compilers, and the common carriers.
While each of these institutions plays an important role
in the system, these roles have relatively little influence
over the policy-making structures. They perform tasks
that lubricate the system in particular ways. But they are
still merely supplying a product or service that carries
with it no significant power to influence the form of what
the industry creates.

Clearly, networks play the pivotal role in determining
television programming, but that role is heavily influenced by the need to satisfy the marketing requirements of advertisers and advertising policies. Although
production houses and broadcast stations appear to play
lesser roles, their impact on the process of creating
programming is nevertheless distinct and tangible. The
description and analysis of the fundamental broadcasting
industry functions and its major institutions provide the
necessary institutional framework for examining the
particular issues of children's television and the possible
consequences of changes in its treatment.

3. The History of Children's Television*

In recent years increased attention has been addressed to children's television from all quarters. Specialized programming has been directed toward cultivating a children's market that can be more effectively exploited by advertisers of children's products. At the same time, public-interest groups, Congress, and the FCC continue to demonstrate increasing concern over the quality and direction of children's programming and the practices and effects of children's advertising. The FCC, in particular, has legal responsibility to ensure that broadcast stations operate in the public interest. At present, the Commission is considering whether it is necessary and desirable to adopt regulatory policy in the area of children's television.

That such regulation might be necessary is not so much a condemnation of broadcasters' motives as it is a recognition that the institutional structure in the broadcasting industries cannot take advantage of the market forces of free entry and effective market competition in meeting the needs of the viewing public. As a "public trustee," the broadcaster is constantly placed in the position of weighing the conflicting objectives of economic profit and public service. He must attempt to make the system serve two generally conflicting masters. The nature of the broadcaster's response in any area of

* With Wendy Ehrlich

33

specific conflict in objectives depends significantly upon his particular position in the institutional structure of the industry. It has been noted already that the individual broadcast station frequently has little or no effective influence over what is produced, broadcast, and advertised over his station.

Because networks are not subject to direct government regulation, it is the broadcast stations that will be subject first and foremost to attempts to create concise standards of broadcast performance. The networks and other institutions within the industry are only indirectly affected by strictures placed upon broadcast stations that they own, are affiliated with, or otherwise influence. That regulation flows backward, as it were, to the medium's reigning institutions involves an obvious irony, for the broadcaster whose actions are directly subject to regulation has very limited control over the overall performance of the complex system upon which he depends for his programs. The broadcaster is most significantly affected by decisions made outside the scope of his own decision-making power. In regulatory terms, the government tells him what he must do in the public interest. In programming and advertising terms, most of the important decisions that define his final range of choice also take place elsewhere. Circumstances where the station retains complete control over all functions of broadcasting—from financing programs, through their production, to their actual broadcast—are rare indeed.

Because decisions concerning policy for children's television usually end rather than begin with the licensee, an analysis of why childrens' programming has evolved the way it has must go beyond an examination of the individual stations to see what they are broadcasting to children. In fact, no institution in the industrial structure of broadcasting—not even the networks—is entirely free to define its own policy and operating objectives without regard to the complex interrelationships with the other segments of the industry. At each level, a number of factors come into play, including the common social, cultural, political, economic, legal, and technical circumstances that limit the scope of their managerial discretion at any point in time.

THE PROMOTIONAL ERA

Because television was a direct outgrowth of radio, inheriting for the most part its industrial structure and business methods, it did not undergo the slow evolution of market development that radio did. Its primary role as a commercial advertising vehicle went unquestioned. Indeed, its initial potential was considered to be its superiority as an instrument for advertising. In addition, since the network structure came to dominate the radio industry, it was easily embraced at the advent of television. Networks exercised extensive control over station schedules almost from the outset. In fact, at this time, the networks, for all intents and purposes, *were* the industry, and performed or controlled all tasks associated with the broadcasting function.

A national network of interconnected affiliates was considered essential for television for the same reason as it was for radio: network formation was the most efficient way to lure sponsors into the medium as a national advertising forum. During the formative years of television, therefore, the economic incentives of the industry were directed toward market development. Of primary initial importance was the creation and establishment of potential audience circulation. In order to put television in an equal competitive position with other media, families had to be motivated to purchase television sets. Programming therefore was directed toward promotion of the medium to insure the greatest public appeal. In fact, this was probably the only time in the history of commercial television when the primary concern of the industry was with programming that would appeal to viewers rather than attract advertising sponsors to television as a forum for selling products. The marketing of television sets and television as a medium took precedence over the marketing of audiences to advertisers.

Treatment of children's programming by the networks during this period also reflects this attempt to attract the potential viewing audience. Specialized children's programming of high quality was viewed as a valuable stimulus to the purchase of television sets. In 1951, for example, the four networks (NBC, CBS, ABC, and the now defunct DuMont) showed twenty-seven hours of children's programming weekly, and primarily at hours when children were inclined to be watching—weekday evenings between six and eight P.M. In 1950, NBC gave children's programming unprecedented priority with the introduction of several programs, such as *Howdy Doody* and *Kukla, Fran, and Ollie.* NBC continued to lead all others in amounts of children's programming until 1957. It is noteworthy that during the early years of television, nearly half of the combined network offerings for children were sustaining, i.e. presented without advertiser sponsorship. In 1949, for example, 42 percent of the offerings were sustaining.[1]

However, the network priority for children's programming was not matched at the local station level. As a carryover from radio practices that resisted the use of recordings, the networks frowned upon the use of film on television. But individual stations acting according to much shorter-run economic objectives found that idle hours not claimed by network option time (the time the stations were obligated to run network fare) could be cheaply filled with old animated short films originally made for the movie theater market as "fillers." As early as 1949 some stations were showing filmed material made especially for first-run television syndication. Stations demonstrated little interest in children as a definable public interest or even as an advertising market category. Children's broadcasting was seldom differentiated from general audience programming by stations, and special efforts in behalf of children were indeed rare.

CONVERSION TO MASS MARKETING

After World War II the television industry developed with phenomenal speed. The demand for station licenses was so great, in fact, that the FCC realized available channel allocations would soon run out if they remained limited to the Very High Frequency (VHF) portion of the radio spectrum. In 1949 the Commission issued a "freeze" order on new station applications to investigate channel allocation policy. Although originally intended to last only ninety days, the freeze actually lasted until April 1952. During this period the number of television sets in use in the U.S. mushroomed from 190,000 to more than 16 million.

With substantially increased circulation, and thus potential advertising revenues, the emphasis in programming shifted from attracting potential viewers to buy television sets toward producing and securing programs that would appeal to sponsors—in other words, from audience development to efficient advertising. By 1954 the sponsors and advertising agencies had firmly taken control of the program schedules of the networks and most stations. According to Les Brown:

> The practice, carried over from radio, had been for advertisers to control time periods at the networks, to fully underwrite the shows presented there, and in many cases to own the properties. This gave them the authority over subject matter and intellectual content and allowed advertisers to impose their standards of production upon the show. The network was no more than a conveyance.[2]

The institutional strength of the advertisers and their agencies naturally was felt in all areas of programming, and both for general and specific audiences. Sponsors were buying programs that acted as efficient vehicles to reach potential customers. Since at this time children were not considered to have a significant influence on buying habits, the result was predictable. Advertisers had no obligation to program specifically for children. Therefore, when it became in their economic interest to do so, they shifted children's programming from the weekday early evening position to afternoon and morning positions. "Prime time" had become too valuable for marketing to mass audiences to be wasted on children. Children's programming was shifted to time-slots where it had an advantage over other kinds of programming as an advertising vehicle. The networks readily went along with such a shift, since it was also in their economic interest to do so. It should be emphasized, however, that at this time the child was not considered an effective marketing device. Advertising directly to the adult was generally viewed as more effective because the adult made the purchases.

Coincident with this shift when children's programming was presented was the rise of the filmed series in 1953. Live network programming was superceded by the now famous "I Love Lucy" format. This change put a premium on the services of artists and technicians formerly allied with the film industry. Both networks and syndicators bought these proliferating film series, and the market was further stimulated by the development of markets for filmed products overseas. By the end of 1954, the live episodic series had become obsolete.

While the period 1953–55 produced what many observers of the industry consider some of the finest television programming for adults ever aired, there are indications that the industry was aware that children were not receiving appropriate attention in their programming. A children's program review committee created by NBC, for example, censored the network's treatment of children's programming on a variety of counts.[3] A Yale study group in 1954 found children's dramatic programs the most violent on the air.[4]

If there were any such reservations about the way children's programming should be handled at the local stations, it certainly was not reflected in their performance. A 1962 article in *Television Age* described the situation in 1953–56: "Little was offered to the local stations besides antique theatrical cartoons or short subjects. Much of this material was dated beyond use, much of it was offensive from today's standards of taste and much of it was of poor print quality; still, in 1953, one industry survey showed 20-25 stations regularly running cartoon shows—the majority of which were getting high ratings."[5]

The mid-1950s brought a renewed interest in television programming for children. In assessing "Children's Programming Trends on Network TV," Maurice Shelby credits sociocultural sanctions on the broadcast industry during this period with the introduction of "such 'quality' programs as *Disneyland*, *Captain Kangaroo*, *Ding Dong School* and others." Although these pressures may have been a contributing factor, the *economic* incentives involved seem even more significant in the new phase of children's programming that followed.

Until 1953 the ABC-TV network was a poor competitor with the two major networks, and DuMont was on its way out. However, its merger with Paramount Theatres gave the network a new footing. While the other networks were still dealing with independent film producers for imitations of *I Love Lucy* and *Dragnet*, ABC management began looking to Hollywood and the major studios as sources for programs. The network's first Hollywood coup was *Disneyland*.

ABC desperately wanted Disney's name and skills; Disney was amenable because of Disneyland, the amusement park. In television, Disney recognized an opportunity for publicity for his park, as well as a means to obtain the capital he still needed to go ahead with it. In a seven-year contract with ABC-Paramount Theatres Inc., he agreed to produce a weekly one-hour television program to be called *Disneyland*, "on which he would be free to promote liberally not only his amusement park but his films." [6] In a separate arrangement, ABC-Paramount agreed to purchase 34-48 percent of the shares of Disneyland, Inc., a firm chartered in 1951, with an option to buy back the shares at par value plus 5 percent a year.

The program *Disneyland* changed not only children's programming, but the whole television program supply market. After it premiered on ABC in October 1954, *Disneyland* quickly rose into Nielsen's top ten, won the Peabody award in 1954 as the best educational television program, and the Emmy award for best adventure series in 1955. On the basis of the Disney experience, Warner Brothers agreed to produce films for ABC for the 1955–56 season, breaking the deadlock that had kept the major Hollywood studios from dealing with their bitter competitive rival, television. But *Disneyland's* acclaim also raised the inevitable question: Why aren't there more programs like it for children? Since *Disneyland* was popular with sponsors, the industry took the cue.

As a result, 1956 was a banner year in the amount of children's programming carried by the networks. Programming for children increased from twenty-two hours in 1955 to thirty-seven hours in 1956. Most of it, however, was still shown during morning and afternoon time periods.[7] Filmed programs for children were pouring out of Hollywood at a prolific rate, and sponsors were interested. Although companies such as General Mills, General Foods, and Kellogg had been selling on children's programs since radio, this new surge of interest attracted many new advertisers who didn't even deal in products used by children. Among the sponsors of the *Mickey Mouse Club* (Disney's new daily program), for example, were Goodrich Tires, Proctor and Gamble, Gold Seal Wax, Minnesota Mining, Bristol Myers, Armour, S.O.S. scouring pads, and Vicks. Apparently, recognized quality in children's programming attracted the support of corporations that desired to identify with good-quality children's programs, and not simply to sell products to an audience of children. In addition, further revenues were being realized from programs popular with children through franchise arrangements with toy manufacturers, which found action telefilms a chief inspiration and selling factor for toys. Such arrangements were made with scores of series, including *Dragnet, Wyatt Earp, Davy Crockett, Ramar of the Jungle,* and so on.

It should be emphasized that this upsurge of interest in children's programming in 1956 was stimulated by economic circumstances. Prior to that time, children's programming had been viewed as unprofitable activity. The Disney experience completely changed the conception of the children's market to one of substantial potential profit for producers, networks, stations, advertisers of children's products, and even others with less direct economic interests in children's television. The result was some programs that were widely acclaimed for their value for children. But more prevalent were programs constructed entirely in the sponsor's selling interests rather than children's.

By 1956–57 it was clear that there was a lot of money to be made in television. As Barnouw describes the situation, "For stations and networks, the road was clear. Film salesmen were lining up, and so were sponsors. Much had been settled, and the boom was on." [8] The economics of promotion had changed into the economics of abundance for the television industry—both networks and stations. The imperatives of sound management now meant exploiting that market advantage for profit. At this point in history, the strategy for achieving that objective primarily involved a two-part formula: prime time and action series.

By now, TV sets had reached a high proportion of

homes and daily viewing was steadily increasing.[9] Intrigued by the opportunities of reaching massive numbers of potential customers, advertising strategy centered around costs per thousands of *viewers* (demographics was not yet part of the television time-buyer's vocabulary). Nielsen rating data indicated that the number of people watching television between 8:00 and 9:00 P.M. was three times greater than between 3:00 and 4:00 P.M., and six times than between 8:00 and 9:00 A.M. The importance of "prime time" to the industry at this time is revealed in testimony by Ely Landau, President of National Telefilm Associates (NTA) during the Television Inquiry hearings before the Senate Committee on Interstate and Foreign Commerce in 1956:

> Those are the hours which command the highest ratings; those are the hours that advertisers vie for. Consequently, those are the most expensive and lucrative hours. Those are the hours that are big-time television, the hours that are known as prime time. Those are the 7:30 to 10:30 evening hours, and they are basically what the shouting is all about.

The programs used to attract the mass audience that sponsors desired were of the action-filled Western/crime-mystery genre. Programs emphasizing action rather than dialogue were much easier and cheaper to translate and dub into foreign languages, which by now was an important consideration. By 1958–59 a television writer could scarcely find a market for any other kind of material.[10]

"FAMILY" PROGRAMMING AND LOCAL STATION INTEREST

The shift in emphasis to the general mass audience did not bode well for programming directed to specialized audiences such as children. Further, when the action-packed formula for prime time was applied to programs intended for children, they invited political censure from Senator Estes Kefauver's Senate Committee hearings on the rising juvenile crime rate, and unfavorable reviews and journal articles. Thus, in the late 1950s, network policy was to absorb the children's television submarket into the larger mass audiences of "eyeballs." Suddenly children's programming was impossible to define. Under no obligation to program specifically for children, it became more profitable to program for the "family" audience in prime time instead. ABC, which had ignited the brief spurt of interest in children's programming with *Disneyland* in pursuit of advertising revenues, was the first to develop this new approach to selling audiences to advertisers, offering sponsors new evening franchises for programs that claimed to deliver ʻa family audience—including, of course, large numbers of children. The other networks again soon followed ABC's lead.

Since non-prime-time children's programming was no longer viewed by the networks as profitable, much of it was dropped after 1956. "In short time, the networks had surrendered the prime children's programming preserve, the 4 to 7 P.M. strip, to the local stations." [11] With sponsors shifting to prime-time family programming, such network children's favorites as the *Mickey Mouse Club, Howdy Doody, Kukla, Fran and Ollie,* and others became network casualties.

For a while, the release of the late afternoon period was to benefit children's programming on the station level. Because the time period had not yet developed any special economic significance for the stations, broadcasters did not yet view it as a potential contributor to profits. They were willing to experiment with it. Since it had been "the children's hour" on the networks for several years, there seemed no reason not to carry over the same idea to the local level.

About this time certain sponsors discovered that local spot-buying on children's programs could be an extremely efficient means of advertising. Usually these programs were based around old theatrical material or reruns of previous network children's programs. *Television Age* noted that: "As film libraries were opened, cartoons came in such abundance that no station worth its salt could afford to get along without a 'children's show'— consisting primarily of a 'personality' to introduce the cartoons and sell the advertiser's products." Local personalities proved to be a formidable selling tool for many sponsors who wanted to talk directly to children. Some manufacturers had even created products specifically for children because of their ability to sell them to children on the local level. This could all be had at the low cost per thousand of between twenty-five and fifty cents. Thus, the local children's shows were able to isolate the local children's audience as a specialized market for more direct and pinpointed advertising of specialized products.

With time periods now available that were previously controlled by the networks, sponsors and stations needed new programming material. The old program supplies were dwindling, as producers of theatrical cartoons could not have anticipated the rate at which television would later consume programs. Old programs were growing increasingly boring and tiresome with constant reuse.

One drawback that had deterred stations from seeking first-run animated material was its cost. Elaborate Disney-style animation was very expensive to create, and took far too long to produce in the amounts required for a television serial. Two animators from the old Metro-Goldwin-Mayer animation unit, William Hanna and Joseph Barbera, saw a way around these obstacles with the limited animation technique, introduced during the post-World War II period in a theatrical short, *Gerald McBoing-Boing.* The technique's applicability to television's need for economy and speed in production had gone unrecognized. In 1958, Hanna-Barbera sold their first made-for-TV series to Kellogg, who then syndicated the program domestically. Neil Compton has observed: "Almost every subsequent development in the genre can be traced back to hints implicit in one or another of the series which made up their first weekly half-hour package—*Huckleberry Hound, Yogi Bear,* and *Pixie and Dixie.*" [12]

NETWORK CONTROL

1960 marked a major shift in control of programming from the sponsors and advertising agencies back to the networks. Barnouw writes:

> No longer would sponsors control periods and determine how they would be used. The network would do the scheduling and let the sponsor know what was available. . . . film producers came to understand that series had to be contracted—'licensed'—to the network, not to the sponsor. The network would determine scheduling and deal with the sponsor.[13]

Although the quiz scandals that came to the surface in 1959 are generally cited as the main reason for the change, there are some very sound managerial reasons for this shift, based on the economic circumstances of the industry.

One important factor was increasing production costs. Sponsors became increasingly hesitant to take the substantial risks of sponsoring a program for which they were singly assuming both the costs of production and time charges to the networks. In an assessment of the reasons for the decline in advertiser-initiated production, a study by A. D. Little concludes that it was unquestionably the sponsors who wanted the change in the assumption of risks; it was not the networks who forced them out of program production.[14]

However, producers were not anxious to assume the risks, which would be substantial when their only outlet was a three-network oligopoly. Furthermore, "friendships" between networks and major production studios made entering the market all the more difficult. As a result, the networks began to finance program production in return for "profit participation." *Broadcasting* magazine's "authoritative but unofficial estimate" of the number of shows on the networks with profit participation in 1960 was well over half. With the expanding international marketplace for television programs, the networks were now assured of revenues, not only from their network operations, but from domestic and international syndication as well.

Considering the increasing financial stakes for which the networks were now competing in prime time, it is apparent that they would eventually have to regain control over their own program schedules or lose ever-increasing amounts of potential profit. Sponsors cared only about the audience ratings their program received; network management was concerned about the whole schedule and the interrelated effects of programs, schedules, audiences, and advertisements. Once again, ABC initiated the change in strategy, introducing the technique of counterprogramming, i.e. designing program schedules in specific response to known or anticipated program schedules of the other networks. Counterprogramming reflected a more sophisticated management approach to marketing audiences. It led to program diversity only when it was profitable to do such programming.

An important element in network prime-time strategy was still the so-called family program. But the networks had begun to take note of some of the new animated material being syndicated by the stations for children's shows. In 1960, Hanna-Barbera was the first to cross the boundary between the afternoon kid-show strip and network prime time, with *The Flintstones,* "an animated cartoon series designed for family viewing." On the heels of its success came a rash of imitations, most of which failed in prime time, but were later put to use in the Saturday morning children's block.

The networks also realized that when they released the prime children's program period to the local stations, they also had cut themselves out of the revenue from those advertisers who were interested in reaching the specialized child audience—primarily the toy industry. Other sponsors, encouraged by their experiences in spot advertising on local children's programming, had discovered a formidable "youth market." Nestle's Quik, for example, was spending 90 percent of its advertising budget on children's television.

Not yet a profit center, children's programming was proving it was capable of carrying its own economic weight on the network schedules. During 1961–62, however, when political sanctions threatened to interfere with the financial boom the industry was then enjoying, children's programming served as the peace offering.

Unlike the relatively mild political rumblings in 1956, caused by Senator Kefauver's hearings, the criticism was now coming from two major government figures, and on two different counts. TV violence was being implicated as contributing to social disorder in Senate hearings on TV and juvenile delinquency, chaired by Senator Thomas Dodd. FCC Chairman Newton Minow was appealing to the industry to provide more that was of positive value—especially for children.

Thus, in 1961 the networks responded by introducing a few informational series for children, such as *Exploring* and *Discovery*. The ideas for many of these shows had existed at the networks for some time, but, according to one producer, "we couldn't get the go-ahead on any of them until Minow." [15] Neil Hickey has described the rationale for programs of this nature as follows: "Each network has its own few enclaves of 'quality' children's programming which it points to when the question arises of whether television is being fully 'responsible' toward its young viewers." [16]

By the end of 1963, programs like *Exploring* and *Discovery* had already fallen by the wayside. FCC Chairman Minow had attempted to pressure the broadcasting industry into making a voluntary moral commitment to improving programming for children. The result was that ad hoc "diversified" programs appeared and died as quickly as they came, once the direct public pressure had receded. Permanent improvement would have required managers of businesses—answerable to stockholders—to establish noneconomic criteria as a permanent part of their decision-making process regarding programming. But responses to temporary pressures cannot be expected to bring permanent changes. Although broadcasters blamed the advertisers for not supporting their "quality" efforts, and advertisers accused the broadcasters of kowtowing to government pressures, the forces of the market prompted broadcasters to subordinate the needs of children to the profit from advertising.

SPECIALIZED AUDIENCES: THE CHILDREN'S MARKET

As television continued to grow, the demand for sponsored time expanded beyond the capacity of the prime-time period. Consequently, other hours began to exhibit profit potential. Sunday afternoon, for example, long an unprofitable "cultural ghetto," was proving it could be profitably mined with professional football. Another profit center had been discovered in weekday television with the housewife market. Although daytime revenues weren't nearly as high as prime-time revenues, production costs were so much less that this period was actually more profitable. In similar manner, another profit center was discovered on Saturday mornings with children's programming.

The compelling force behind the recognition of children as a specialized audience was the advertisers' discovery of the youth market, i.e. "the $50 billion opportunity." [17] Inspired by the Kennedy administration, the accent on youth had infiltrated all spheres of American activity, including the demand for consumer goods. Barnouw observes: "Saturday mornings, once regarded as a time for do-good programs to please women's groups, were becoming profitable for a different reason. Toy manufacturers were adopting year-round rather than seasonal advertising schedules and were the main Saturday morning sponsors, backing a parade of animated films, largely violent." [18]

The field was not limited to toys, however. By 1965, advertisers of other products for young children, such as candy and breakfast foods, had discovered that their targets could be reached as effectively on Saturday mornings as in prime time, and much more cheaply. According to the Nielsen ratings for that period, advertisers could reach a thousand children in network weekend shows for $1.00, whereas weekdays they would only reach 286 children for their dollar, and in prime time only 133 kids.[19]

The new use of Saturday morning was as popular with the networks as it was with the sponsors, and for similar economic reasons. Following the economic principles of daytime television, production expenses were minimized and profits increased. In addition, there were economic advantages not available in prime time: twice as much advertising time, more use of reruns, and lower discounts on advertising rates in the summer.

Producers of children's programs were anxious to supply the networks with new programs in response to the new demand. Network distribution had several major advantages over syndication for the producer. And technical developments at the time were making placement on the networks even more desirable. One was the race to utilize color on television. Another was the further development of the limited-animation cartoon style. By 1962, the Hanna-Barbera organization—at the peak of the animation-for-TV roster—was said to be reaping an annual profit of over a million dollars from merchandising tie-ins alone.[20] Imitations of their cartoons abounded. By 1967, the three networks were engaged in increasingly intense competition for the attention of the weekend-television-viewing child, which had developed into a multimillion-dollar market in network television alone.

Children's television had emerged as a full contender

in the ratings and revenue competition between the
networks. As this market became more and more lucrative, the profit opportunities for competitive market
shares increased. The payoff for gaining or losing in the
ratings was becoming increasingly great. Hence, the
children's schedule was attracting more and more careful
attention as a device for profitably delivering child
audiences to specific advertisers. And as the economic
stakes increased, the risks of deviating from the pursuit of
strict economic objectives brought a concurrent decrease
in managerial flexibility. Now the potential profits that
would be foregone by not fully exploiting the children's
markets for advertising had become too great to permit
much experimentation.

As in prime time, the lucrative nature of the market
elevated counterprogramming as an important aspect of
competitive strategy. In order to counterprogram the
children's schedule successfully, the networks had to
retain complete control over program placement. A
practice known as "routining" became an integral part of
the network's job. Routining, in essence, is the delivery of
specific subclassifications of an audience market to
specific sponsors for that subclassification. For children, it
means delivering the right program to the right age-
group of children at the right time of the morning—to
attract a maximum audience for sponsors. It is creating
an even more specialized audience that advertisers can
exploit more directly and efficiently. A principle concern
of the networks became building a continuing audience
flow throughout the morning, moving from programs for
younger children early in the morning to those appealing
primarily to older children later, when they controlled
the television dials.

This control over programming and scheduling was

facilitated by the decrease in advertiser-owned series for many of the same reasons as in prime time. (In 1967, for example, all sponsored weekend network children's programming was bought on a participating basis or multiple sponsorship.) Because of increased production costs for children's programs due to the insurgence of color and the demand for first-run, made-for-television material, programs had to be broadcast several times over an extended period to amortize expenses, a tremendous risk for a single sponsor. Also, whereas brand identification with certain programs used to be a desired objective, advertisers interested in the children's market now found it more financially feasible to take advantage of new network "package minutes" and spread their commercials around the entire kiddie circuit on weekends.

Children's television had become a seller's market for advertising time and a buyer's market for programming. Operating at the crossroads of the market, the networks were in a position of substantial monopoly power, both in selling audiences and buying programs—market power that they attempted to use generally to their fullest profit-maximizing potential. Traditional children's advertisers—for toys, candy, breakfast foods, and soft drinks—were vying with each other for time on the network children's weekend schedules. The financial success of the children's market for networks and advertisers prompted advertising agencies to specialize in researching the influence of children on family buying habits for all product categories, and applying the new market information toward attracting new advertising accounts in children's television.

Network control over content in children's television became increasingly powerful at this time. Since advertisers were no longer identified with the programs on which they advertised, they were not as sensitive to the many criticisms of the trends in children's programming and advertising. The enormous profit potential, and the corresponding economic risks of failing to respond fully and effectively to advertiser needs, tended to inhibit experimentation and decision-making flexibility all down the line, from networks to producers and stations. For producers, this meant that they had to conform more than ever to directives of the networks. Joseph Barbera is quoted as stating, in 1967: " 'We're doing monster stuff mainly,' . . . Comic-book fiction, super heroes, and fantasy. Not out of choice, you understand. It's the only thing we can sell to the networks, and we have to stay in business." [21] The networks could control programming best, of course, by assigning its production to the loyal suppliers. By 1967, most first-run children's programming was supplied by a half-dozen production houses.

The economic evolution of children's television has passed through several very distinct phases of development. During the promotional era, it represented a source of program differentiation that helped stimulate long-term industry growth by providing incentives for families to purchase television sets, and thereby expanding potential audiences. When television-set penetration approached saturation and ratings determined broadcast revenues, audiences were conceived of as reasonably homogeneous mass markets of "eyeballs." Children's programming lost its previous specialized identity because it was not warranted on the basis of profit-making potential in comparison with mass audiences for the same time-slots. Finally, children as a specialized audience were rediscovered in true economic terms, i.e. as a profitable product for sale to specialized advertisers.

It is apparent that recognition of the children's television market as an enormously profitable one has brought changes in the distribution of economic power in the industry. Control over industry developments has been concentrated in the networks, shifting from the advertisers, program producers, and stations. Increasing centralized control and monopoly power in the networks has paralleled the development of profit opportunities that could best be exploited through dominant market-managers "at every stage of the creative process from the initial script to the final broadcast." [22] Market development has been directed toward tailoring the service of delivering audiences to the particular interests of advertisers. Thus, the delivery of general purpose audiences is giving way to an increasing role for specialized children's audiences.

But this response of broadcasting to the specialized needs and requirements of advertisers is precisely what has led to the avalanche of complaints about abuses in children's programming and advertising, and which has raised the children's television issue to the level of public policy determination. On the one hand, the problem of excessive monopoly power by the networks raises important questions about the role of competition and antitrust policy in networking and network ties to program production and broadcast stations. But more important for the present study is the impact of specialization in child audiences upon children's programming and advertising practices, the unique characteristics of which are pursued in the next chapter.

4. The Unique Characteristics of Children's Television

Chapter 2 outlined the fundamental economic character-istics of the production, distribution, and broadcast functions in the television industry and of the institutions that perform them. It is within this basic model of the industry that children's television operates, subject to many of the same fundamental economic forces at work within the industry at large. Yet children's television does have unique characteristics that differ significantly from the broader framework of the industry model. Some of the institutions described in chapter 2 have peculiarly differentiated forms that have arisen in response to these unique characteristics.

These specialized forms may reflect either ways in which the child-audience differs in its viewing habits, sensibilities, and perceptions from the adult audience, or ways in which the child-audience is perceived by adver-tisers, networks, program producers, syndicators, or broadcast station managers as a specialized economic market. But the characteristics of the child-audience as a specialized market for advertisers *need have no relationship* to those attributes which distinguish child viewers from more mature audiences, and which would provide a basis for designing children's programs for the purpose of enriching children. At various stages in the development of commercial television, the child has been believed by broadcasters and advertisers to have various kinds of influence over important decisions, such as television-set purchase, program selection, and family product purchases. These conceptions have had a major impact upon industry practices and the direction of development in children's television.

THE CHILDREN'S MARKET

Specialization in children's television has developed in several of the industry's functions, as the particular characteristics of the child-audience as a profitable market for commercial exploitation has been recognized. As in the development of all specialized markets, once the specific market specialization is recognized in the demand for the final product—in this case, the demand for child-audiences by advertisers—it tends to breed specialization at other points in the production process, as the industry responds to new potentials for more efficient supply and increased profit. Over the past several years this process has been evolving in children's television at an increasing rate. From a starting point of recognition of children's audiences and advertisers, an entire children's television industry has been created, with specialization throughout its various functions and institutions.

Exploiting the characteristics of specialized audiences requires that traditional mass-media market indicators, such as the total number of viewers in an audience, give way to a focus on the component parts of those audiences. Instead of seeking exposure to a large, undifferentiated audience and a relatively low response rate to an advertisement, advertisers in specialized markets seek a relatively high response rate from a smaller, selected audience. Thus, specialized programming and advertising to children permits the tailoring of the audience delivery service to the specific audiences that children's advertisers desire. In a marketing sense, it can be much more efficient than serving up random conglomerations of undifferentiated mass audiences.

Once the basis for market specialization is recognized, the differentiation from mass markets can, of course, be cultivated by the seller of audiences. This is accomplished through business strategy for determining programming content, the time and frequency of program schedules, the sequence of programs, as well as general promotion and virtually all other aspects of supplying demographically specific audiences. This market cultivation has come to characterize children's, and particularly weekend, programming.

This evolving specialization and cultivation of demographically pure markets can be expected to continue in children's television as long as the profit opportunities for such market segmentation continue to exist. Forecasts of the potential market for specialized child-audience advertising all tend to indicate that exploitation of this market for its full profit potential by advertisers and broadcasters will not occur for some time to come. In this regard, marketing in children's television is just nearing the end of its stage of embryonic growth and getting ready for substantial additional growth, as more sophisticated techniques of market segmentation, cultivation, and advertising are brought to bear on it. As the potential profit of the children's market becomes greater and greater, it also becomes more and more economical to bring more sophisticated techniques for market analysis and more managerial time and effort to pinpointing the precise characteristics of the children's markets and submarkets so that advertisers can exploit them to their full potential.

ADVERTISERS AND NETWORKS

Advertising is a $4 billion-a-year industry, and more than $400 million a year is spent to convince children to buy. As noted in chapter 2, advertising agencies have become increasingly specialized, with time buyers and market researchers working to help budget these large sums of money most efficiently. In children's advertising, specialized youth-marketing agencies are now probing youth markets in great detail—going far beyond traditional ratings values—in developing detailed marketing and advertising placement strategies. *Mediascope* lists over fifteen such agencies specializing in the youth market in New York City alone. Robert B. Choate, chairman of the Council on Children, Media, and Merchandising, has recently described the stated objectives and activities of these specialized youth-marketing agencies in testimony before the U.S. Senate. He stated:

> Today, in motivational research houses across the country, children are being used in laboratory situations to formulate, analyze, polish, compare, and act in advertisements designed to make other children salesmen within the home. Armed with one-way mirrors, hidden tape recorders, and inobtrusive videorecorders, professionally trained psychologists and experts in child behavior note every motion, phrase, and other indication of children's responses.[1]

The advertisements for children's audiences tend to be loud, bright, and action-oriented, and are integrated as closely as possible into the program in order to reduce the probability of losing the child viewer's attention at the time of the advertising break. The traditional fade to black before commercials is often not used, so that the child, who lacks the perceptual discriminatory power of the adult, will not recognize the difference between program and commercial. This process is facilitated, of course, if the program is designed and planned to merge with the advertisement. For example, animated advertisements are used with animated programs. Maximum impact is achieved by the ad when the child is deceived into believing that the promotion of certain products is simply part of his entertainment. Advises one youth-advertising specialist: "TV can be highly effective for the preschool group. With a good program and a good commercial, you can command 60 seconds of total interest—the child's eyes will remain riveted on the screen. But preschoolers are famous dial twisters. The program has to provide action and adventure, the way animated cartoons do, to involve the viewer, and so does the commercial." [2]

Children's advertising is also tailored to the market in other ways. The frequent repetition of ads reflects consideration of the relatively short memory spans of children.[3] The ads cater to peculiar needs, anxieties, and status concerns of children, exploiting peer group competitiveness to stimulate desires for the child to be the first, the best, the hero, the most popular, etc. For example, Helitzer and Heyel observe with regard to the status concerns of children:

Children, just like their parents, are highly status conscious. Commercials that appeal to the desire for stature in the child world are highly effective. Children respond to appeals that carry the promise of making them a better person, or smarter, or stronger, or someone that is growing up faster than the other kids.

The infamous phrase, 'be the first kid on your block,' has been subject to considerable criticism—both seriously and in not-so-funny jest. However, in the children's marketplace, this idea is a tested and proven persuader. Every child strives to get an edge on his contemporaries, to be first. One-upmanship is far from being an exclusively adult phenomenon.[4]

We have noted that the advertisers in the children's television market are heavily concentrated in such products as cereals, candies, snack foods, toys, and until recently, vitamins. This high degree of specialized marketing insures that the advertising on children's shows has filtered down to specific products that have demonstrated a unique capability for influencing the behavior of the child viewer and the purchasing habits of his parents.

Both children's advertising practices and the types of products advertised clearly indicate that the thrust of children's advertising is toward an immediate impression followed by a quick sale of the product. This, of course, exploits the vulnerability of children's first impressions and their immediate emotional responses. It has led to substantial fluctuations in the demand for advertising minutes, with the greatest demands preceding holiday occasions. It has created an unprecedented advertising boom just before Christmas, when the combination of the holiday spirit and the normal techniques for children's advertising make child viewers and their parents especially vulnerable, and therefore the probable effectiveness of such advertising is at its peak.

The specialization of advertisers in children's television also has become media specialization for some products when some firms—for example, Nestle's Quik and some toy companies—have come to spend extremely high proportions of their total media advertising budget on children's television. The ability to reach a large number of child viewers at a relatively low cost per thousand, through "scatter plans" on network and local programs, has stimulated an unusual degree of specialization in these advertisers' media budgets. It clearly indicates substantial success in stimulating the child to serve successfully as a conduit to adults for purchase of the advertised products.

The specialization in children's television by certain advertisers has led to other related institutional developments. The acquisition of toy manufacturing concerns by several of the large cereal manufacturers is one example. The impact of televised toy advertising on the toy retailing industry and the product produced has received some attention in recent Federal Trade Commission (FTC) hearings.[5] Although character merchandising tie-ins and premium offers existed long before television, children's television advertising has helped give firms specializing in these practices new institutional stature. Helitzer and Heyel counsel manufacturers on how to pick "the right character for your product":

> But in our opinion, if you want to create your own hard-hitting spokesman to children, the most effective route is the superhero—miracle worker. He certainly can demonstrate food products, drug items, many kinds of toys, and innumerable household items.[6]

They go on to emphasize:

> The character should be adventurous. And he should be on the right side of the law. A child must be able to mimic his hero, whether he is James Bond, Superman

or Dick Tracy; to be able to fight and shoot to kill without punishment or guilt feelings.[7]

The effectiveness of children's television as an advertising medium has been influenced by the ability of broadcasters to create a "ghetto" of child audiences by cultivating a television time-slot where children can be selected and isolated for advertisers without conflicting with other potential audience groups. The most profitable time period for children's television is when the next-most profitable, alternative kind of programming for using that period is a very distant second. In fact, child audiences may be the only profitable weekend-morning audiences that can be sold for many broadcasters. However, if the cultivated child audience on weekend mornings is at all substitutable for child audiences in other time-slots, then even if children's television were the most profitable type of program at another time period than Saturday morning, it might still be, after total system effects are considered, to the financial interests of the broadcasters to confine children's programming to the children's ghetto that has already been cultivated. Under these circumstances, other time-slots having potential audiences that are reasonably close to child audiences in profitability can be pursued without shifting child audiences away from weekend mornings.

A basic marketing technique for cultivating specialized audience markets in children's television is "routining," as discussed in chapter 3. The practice of routining is one that is based upon a more detailed breakdown of submarket groups for greater market specialization. Programming and advertising are not simply planned and developed in individual time-slots for individual child audiences, but larger system planning is undertaken for the sequence of programs and advertisements over the entire children's ghetto period. This enables programs and advertisements to be specifically responsive to the particular age-group of children that will be controlling the television dial at a particular point in time during the children's ghetto hours. For example, programming and advertising can reflect the results of detailed market research which may indicate, for example, that before 9:00 A.M. on Saturdays, two- to five-year-olds control the dial; from 9:00 to 10:00 A.M., six- to eleven-year-olds control the dial; and after 10:00 A.M., twelve-year-olds control the dial. Helitzer and Heyel point out the effectiveness of the network scheduling strategy for children's programming:

> In any average minute on a Saturday morning after eight o'clock, regardless of the program, there are 10 million pairs of children's eyes glued to the set, and before the day is over, 75 percent of all children in all TV households will have watched some program.[8]

On the basis of detailed demographic information, programs, advertisements, and advertisers can specialize within the children's market. In addition, advertising rates can be adjusted accordingly, to reflect such detailed market information as the fact that fewer "impressions," or repetitions, are needed to get an advertiser's message across to older children. And as market research gets better, it will bring improvements in the ability to pinpoint ads most efficiently and effectively to "reach" specific subgroups of children, and to employ advertising techniques that will make the most "impression." Also, ads are sometimes designed to feed on one another, piggyback style, in terms of their impressions on children.

A serious problem that develops with much of children's programming is that its short-run focus and constant repetition create a continuing need for new products and new ads to sell them. This leads to an artificial turnover in both ads and products, and incidental differentiations must be blown up into monumental changes if all of the industrial institutions in the process are to continue performing these functions that have a short-run effect.

Norman S. Morris has pointed out that:

> Children are continually sold fads and useless toys because the advertiser knows perfectly well tiny kids are impractical, open to suggestion, and fickle. Evidence of this fact can be found in the playroom of just about any household where children have grown up. The plastic airplane models that flew but once, the bugles that blew perhaps a couple of times, the little girl's footsies that have never been worn. Hard sell and repetition are the usual techniques of moving fad merchandise, but such oversell can backfire, drawing irritation from parents and children alike.[9]

However, we must emphasize that an industrial process based on advertising with a short-run emotional effect and the sale of fads and other short-lived merchandise requires at least a continual replenishment, and sometimes continuing growth, of new products and new ads for its survival. All the institutions in the process have a vested interest in keeping it running at accelerating rates, no matter what the product and no matter how artificial the advertising.

The specialization in children's television by the advertisers who have zeroed in on that market, and by the broadcasters who have segmented and isolated a concentrated children's audience to sell to advertisers, although generally profitable for both groups, has also created some problems for them. A serious "traffic jam" has developed, where several advertisers selling the same types of product want to advertise to children at the same time. This can create scheduling problems if the advertiser insists on the same "product protection" he can count on in other programs. The rule of thumb generally is a fifteen-minute separation between competing products; on children's programs, competing messages are sometimes placed back-to-back.

The sheer amount of advertising allowed on children's programs has created such a condition of commercial "clutter," that some advertisers are reverting to program sponsorship for specials or even series, where, as in the early days of television, they do not have to compete with other advertisers on that program, and they can determine the amount and frequency of commercial interruption. Health-Tex is the notable example of an advertiser that sponsors programs for children, but solely on an institutional basis. In 1971, Ideal Toy Corporation announced it was abandoning advertising on weekend children's programs in favor of the family programs reaching a mixed parent-and-child audience. The move was an effort to gain exclusiveness for its toy advertising messages. The Broadcast Advertisers Report (BAR) figures for 1972, however, indicate that most children's advertisers still prefer to scatter their messages around the children's programming "ghetto."

NETWORKS AND PRODUCERS

There is also considerable specialization in the production of children's television programming. Major network suppliers of children's programming such as Hanna-Barbera, De-Patie–Freleng, and Walt Disney, are primarily known for their involvement in children's production activity. The firms that have chosen to specialize in this sphere of production have responded to the developing demand for their product, and are oriented to the needs of their buying institutions. The buyers of children's programming, however, as has already been indicated, are not necessarily oriented toward the needs of children.

The high concentration of control in most areas of programming by the networks is paralleled in children's program production. As the children's advertising market continues to grow in potential profitability, the networks are assuming an even greater influence over the entire process of delivering programs and audiences to advertisers. This substantially closed market for children's programs has evolved from the necessity of networks to control the process in order to fully exploit the profit potential of the children's television market. It is essential to market control and profit maximization. It has no necessary relationship either to the development of programming to meet the needs of children, or even to the maintenance of a competitive program-production market that at least provides some reasonable opportunity for entry to the market by new producers of innovative programming. Network monopsony power (concentration of control over product sales in the hands of a few buyers) over the children's program production market restricts and directs the level of competition that exists between producers, and the creative autonomy of those who have been able to gain entry into the marketplace. It also creates significant barriers to entry for any new firms, which will have great difficulty surviving unless they can sell to the few buyers who dominate the market.

The number of network suppliers for regularly scheduled children's series is limited. According to a study
conducted as part of the Surgeon General's study on
Television and Social Behavior, in the 1970–71 season, "Three
major and several small independent companies now
share the 12 hours of [network] Saturday morning
children's programming."[10] The situation is similar for
the current 1972–73 season, with the leader, Hanna-Barbera, producing a minimum of eight half-hours of *new*
programming weekly for the networks' Saturday morning schedules, out of a total of approximately twenty-two
half-hours being filled with new productions.

The terms of development for new children's programming provide continuity to those producers already
producing programs for the networks, and act as a
barrier to entry for those struggling to break into the
market. The typical network contract for a children's
program series is for seventeen half-hour episodes, with a
guarantee that each of these will be used six times over
two years. After their initial run, the network might
contract for several new episodes of an especially popular
program. Although there are indications that the networks are reducing their involvement in such long-range
commitments for children's programs, this general pat-
tern still prevails and tends to result in a system where
children's programs are rerun regardless of the success of
the first run, thus minimizing the risk of financial failure
for the producer.

In children's programming in particular, therefore, the
networks are less apt to award such a long-term commitment to an untested producer. Generally, pilots are not
required for animated programs; only the little-known
independent houses are forced to make an entire animated film before it is sold. Instead, animated series are
bought and sold on the basis of story-board presentations,

with some recorded voices as illustration. Another advantage to the established network suppliers is the use of the "spin-off" in children's programming, where new characters are introduced in a segment of an established series in lieu of producing a pilot.[11]

This system not only benefits the producer by "selling" new program series to the network; it also has huge benefits once the programs are released for syndication. Similar series can then be grouped as a children's package, providing the number of episodes that stations find desirable for program "strips." For example, 20th-Century TV, a major children's program syndicator, sold the 120 episodes of *Batman* in a package with the 26 episodes of *Green Hornet*, thereby providing stations with 146 episodes, or a full year's supply of compatible children's programming for "stripping."

Perhaps the most blatant way in which the networks foreclose competition in children's program production is by simply buying an idea the network thinks has merit from a small house without a proven track record, and awarding its development and production to a larger house with proven capabilities for the kind of production quality the network depends on, and for predictable delivery. The networks argue that they just cannot take the risk of dealing with an untested newcomer, unaccustomed to the network's demand for prolific yet speedy production. The effect of this monopsony power in the programming market is that it denies imaginative and innovative efforts at programming reasonable access to viable markets except at enormous risks to the producer. In most circumstances, the great majority of the market for his product is simply foreclosed to the innovative producer.

The outstanding exception to this institutional arrangement in which production houses generally have to accept dictated content decisions is Disney Studios. Just as the scarcity of space gives networks a superior bargaining position over most producers, so the uniqueness of the Disney mystique, with a built-in public following, gives the Disney studios superior bargaining position over the networks. The networks must therefore take Disney productions on Disney studios' terms.

However, the evidence indicates that the other production houses function as little more than cost-plus operations that provide programs at whatever costs are budgeted by the network. Hence, program quality becomes the variable factor in production, as production processes are adapted to budget constraints. This has meant factory-line production scheduling, the churning out of standardized, homogeneous products, and the minimization of programming costs and risks.

Michael Eisner, vice president of Program Development and Children's Programming for ABC-TV, has observed:

> For years, many television series for children were ground out on an assembly line that by its very nature could produce only mediocrity. Men and women were paid perhaps $250 a script to contrive endlessly repetitious situations and characters. With a file of standard plots on hand they ground out "The Circus Story" or "The Jungle Story" simply shifting a new set of characters for each series in and out of the same basic story concepts. . . . Action and adventure cartoons often made aggressive or violent confrontations a part of plot development. . . . in children's programs

all failure happens before millions of people. Every word that's written, every foot that's shot, everything goes on the screen. Our responsibility is clearly drawn —we have to have the ability to abandon at script stage.[12]

Only recently has the network claimed to pay writers an amount for a children's script commensurate with other programming.

Costs have been further minimized through the practically exclusive use of animated cartoon programming for children on Saturday mornings. Since animators do not accrue royalties, as do live actors, the costs of rerunning a program are greatly reduced. The use of limited animation also helps—requiring perhaps only four drawings per frame rather than sixty-four. All cartoon programming currently on weekend daytime schedules uses the limited animation technique—some more limited than others.

Another cost-cutting technique involves the production of short animated segments that can be fit interchangeably into any episode in a series. When the program is a spin-off of another series, even more segment re-use is possible, confirming one writer's suspicions that "many of these so-called new animated series . . . are spliced-together leftovers, film clips from old shows, as in the case of Wacky Races. It is a practice that saves inspiration, spares creative thought, and just incidentally saves scoopfuls of money." [13] As mechanized animation through the use of computers is perfected, further savings in cost can be anticipated. This technique is already widely used for animated commercials, with estimated cost reductions at half of what manual animation costs. Also, in recognition of the worldwide market for children's programs, cost minimization often leads to minimization of English-language words for international expletives and the general substitution of action for words.

Unlike adult programming, most children's programs are rerun indefinitely, regardless of the success of the first run, because the child audience is not as discriminating as adult audiences, and consists of a hard core of cultivated time-slot rather than program viewers. Hence, total failures are infrequent, risks are minimal, amortization schedules can be based upon more showings, and there is generally a substantial market in syndication after first-run showings. The unique characteristics of children's programs make them ideal low-cost fillers of time-slots that can't be used for the profitable selling of other viewer audiences to advertisers.

SYNDICATION

As discussed in chapter 2, syndication has developed as a supplement and/or an alternative to networking under certain circumstances. Most UHF and independent VHF stations obtain the majority of their programming through syndication, and many of these stations air more hours of children's programming than the network affiliated stations. Almost all stations utilize some form of syndicated children's programming, filling in the interstices of the market left by the network segments.

An old practice that has been revived is advertiser-syndication, also called "reciprocal trade" or "barter," in which a company will supply a program in return for a certain number of "free" commercials on the program; the station gets the program "free" as well, obtaining the remaining commercial time in which to insert its own commercials. No cash changes hands—hence the name "barter." This practice is growing particularly attractive to some advertisers appealing to the child market, because of its premium of exclusivity. Pinpoint strategies for identifying markets and reaching them have gathered advertisers of similar products all seeking advertising time at the same times, on the same programs. Commercial clutter and lack of product protection in children's programming—often causing chaos and confusion rather than "impressions" on the minds of their targeted audience—have become a source of great concern to these advertisers.

Off-network reruns, however, form the life-blood of syndication. Network programs originally intended for adults or family viewing, are widely syndicated and time-slotted for rerun appeal to children. In fact, with the release of the 7:30–8:00 P.M. weekday time period by the networks to the stations, the decline in network, juvenile-oriented, "family" programming usually scheduled in that period will almost certainly increase the value of existing syndication properties of this kind. Children make the ideal audience for syndicated repeats. They don't seem to mind having seen a program before, programming for them does not "date" as easily, and the audience replenishes itself every year.

BROADCAST STATIONS

Local station production of children's programming is not a large percentage of all locally produced programming, and in fact, "despite pressures from the FCC and consumer groups, children's programming has declined as a percentage of all locally-produced programming, as the past four years indicate: 1969, 13.5%; 1970, 6.8%; 1971, 8.1%; and 1972, 6.6%." [14] Some stations produce no local children's programming at all, relying only on the weekend feeds from the networks or on syndicated cartoons.[15] Although some locally produced programs have received a justified amount of favorable attention in recent years with renewed public interest in the area, the "typical" local children's production is characterized by the "host show"—primarily a device for low-cost advertising for local merchants.

Some of the problems in attempting quality children's production on the local level are illustrated by the case of *Jabberwocky*, produced by WCVB in Boston. In order to attract advertising revenues commensurate with the station's investment, the program ideally should be scheduled at a time when it can reach a good number of its targeted audience—school-age children. The weekday 3:30–6:00 time periods, however, were considered by station management as too crucial for the housewife market to interrupt with juvenile programming. Until recently, therefore, the program was shown at 9:00 A.M. on weekdays, where it could only attract a low rating.

The economics of syndication make it prohibitive for most stations to attempt to amortize their production costs through sales to other stations. The notable exception is the group-owned stations, some of which have responded to pressure from the public and the FCC for better children's programming with some ambitious local children's production—syndicated among the group, and perhaps other stations.

In terms of overall volume of children's programming shown, however, the independent stations generally lead the network affiliates.[16] The number of UHF stations licensed to operate in the 1960s increased due to the

All-Channel Act, which requires that all television sets sold in interstate commerce be capable of receiving both VHF and UHF signals. For UHF independent stations competing against network affiliates for a share of the audience and advertising dollars, children's programming has proven to be an effective means to counterprogram. In the late 1960s many VHF stations, counseled by demographics-minded station representatives, abandoned children's programming on the late weekday afternoons and programmed for appeal to the 18–39-year-old "housewife market." An independent VHF or UHF station in the market would usually fill the void thus created and become known as the "children's station," showing endless reruns of old network programs with appeal to children.

Most stations show some type of syndicated children's programming, often in marginal time periods. Some programs are first-run productions such as *Bozo's Place* or *The New Zoo Revue.* In some cases—the best-known program being *Romper Room*—the program *format* is actually syndicated: local television "teachers" conduct the program under the close supervision of Romper Room, Inc. Most syndicated children's programming aired by local stations, however, is the packaged reruns of old network series, and the "short subject" theatrical films (usually animated), frequently used as segments of locally produced "host shows."

THE CHANGING CONCEPTION OF CHILDREN

The unique characteristics of children's television depend upon the perspective of children held by those who control programming and advertising decisions. To a significant degree, the evolution of children's television can be traced to the changing conception of the influence of children over the television dial for program selection and over family purchase habits. Directly related to the latter is the advertisers' idea of the effects of advertising on children rather than adults. Over the past quarter-century, we have seen the perceived role of the child change from one of relatively little influence over programming and family purchase decisions to one of major influence. Also, we are seeing a continuously developing awareness on the part of advertisers, market researchers, and broadcasters of the unique vulnerabilities of children to advertising and the potential role of children as lobbyists for the advertiser in the home.

During the promotional era of television development, the primary objective of the industry was to achieve basic market penetration by encouraging the sale of television sets. Children were soon recognized as one of several specialized classifications of viewers for which good programming could stimulate television-set purchases. There is no indication, however, that the child was conceived of as an influential force of any significance in the decision to purchase a set. Rather, attractive children's programming was viewed as one of several reasons why adults would be prompted to purchase a television set. It will be recalled that during the promotional era, a significant proportion of children's programs were unsponsored. Then, the child was not viewed as having any special influence over family decisions to purchase television sets, select programs, or purchase advertised products.

Once market penetration of television sets was achieved, the focus of attention for viewer programming and viewer purchase decisions was directed toward adults. Specialized, good-quality children's programming was no longer needed to sell sets. Adults were presumed to be making the fundamental decisions relating to family program selection and product purchases. Children's audiences were considered only in the sense that adults might view some children's programs with favor, and perhaps watch some children's programming along with their children. The adult was thought of as being in virtually complete control of product-purchase decisions, and in dominant control over program selection. This is illustrated in Figure 3. The child plays no significant role in the family decision-making relating to program selection or product-purchase decisions.

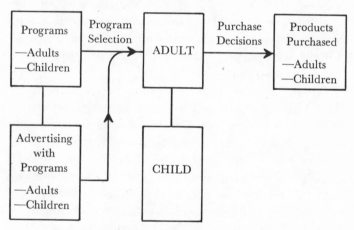

Figure 3. Commercial Television Directed to Adult
Purchase Decisions

This system is directed to the adult family decision-maker. Given this conception of viewer decision-making, advertising to children is an unprofitable activity. It is not part of this decision-making system at all. To the extent that the child participates in the adult audience, the presence of his "eyeballs" are better than their absence because there may be some marginal effects if adults and children watch television together. It was this conception of child and adult viewers that prompted the introduction of family programming and suddenly made children's programming impossible to define.

As commercial television developed further, the image of the child viewer changed. Broadcasters and advertisers recognized that the child may have substantial influence over program selection, although not over product purchases. Accepting this idea of child influence, programming decisions must pay special attention to the child's selection of the program, but above all it must not drive away the adult viewer who is the objective of the advertising messages. Thus, under this view we are still in an era of family programming and mass marketing of eyeballs, with particular attention being paid to the new role of children in program selection.

The major shift to specialization in children's programming came with a perception of the child having significant influence over the purchase of certain products, i.e. those that he personally desires, e.g. toys, sweets, cereals, etc. His substantial control over program selection and significant influence over the purchase of children's products now made it profitable to direct both programming and advertising decisions at the child.

However, advertising to the child must be much more powerful than advertising to adults, because children don't actually make the purchases. The child must be turned into an active lobbyist for the advertiser if the purpose of the effort—to sell the advertised products—is to be achieved. However, the child is much more vulnerable to the motivational effects of advertising. Thus, the child becomes a special-interest medium of advertising. To make the child effective in this role, it becomes desirable in some instances to plan children's programming to repel and exclude adults so that they will be unaware of the nature of the advertising effort, and therefore less resistant to their children's lobbying.

It is this objective that has spawned the weekend "ghetto" of children's programming. And it is against this objective, its practices and its consequences, that criticisms of children's television are leveled, and against which the ACT petition to the FCC requests the formulation of regulatory policy.

THE CHILD AS THE MEDIUM

Current practices in advertising, and in motivational research for advertising, indicate that the industry's concept of children is shifting yet again. Preparation is being made for the final step in the process of changing the focus of commercial television from adults to children. The idea is developing that children may be the best targets of advertising for adult products. At least for many products, advertising to a child lobbyist is viewed as more effective than advertising directly to the purchaser.

William D. Wells has observed:

When other family members have no special brand preferences, and when the mother regards all brands as more or less the same, the preferences expressed by children are apt to determine what the whole family gets. From the advertiser's point of view, then, there are good reasons for being interested in how children think and what they do.[17]

Helitzer and Heyer note:

Children can be very successful naggers. By and large parents quite readily purchase products urged upon them by their youngsters. In Helitzer Advertising's research, it was found that a parent will pay 20 percent more for an advertised product with child appeal—even when a less expensive, non-advertised product is no different.

They go on to emphasize:

Mothers surveyed indicate that because their children ask for specific products and brands, they spend an average of $1.66 more per household weekly. Thus 'child-power' adds at least $30 million weekly, or $1.5 billion annually, to grocery retail sales—just to make Junior happy.

And finally, pointing toward the future, they observe:

With the direct visual medium provided by television, manufacturers of such products as food, drug, and toiletry items and clothing can advertise and sell as effectively to these youngsters as can the makers of candy, gum, toys and games. The biggest mistake being made in basic advertising strategy today is aiming exclusively at the parents of this market segment, with adult appeals that sail completely over the youngsters' heads.[18]

This evolving perspective of the role of children in commercial broadcasting by broadcasters and advertisers fundamentally alters the direction and structure of advertising and program production decisions. The primary role of the child is not as a viewer, but as a medium. In contrast to Figure 3, this is illustrated in Figure 4.

It will be noted that the child has become, in this

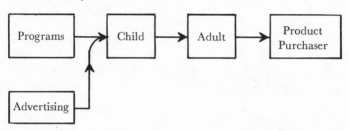

Figure 4. Commercial Television Directed to Child
Lobbyists

model, an integral part of the mechanism for marketing to adults. The marketing team is no longer television advertising, but the powerful triumvirate of advertising, television, and the intrafamily sales force, the children. As this new structure of marketing media is developed and improved, children can be expected to become more efficiently and effectively integrated into this marketing system.

For those who are concerned about advertising and programming practices in commercial children's television today, the future does not look bright. The unique characteristics of this specialized market make children natural targets for profitable integration into the television advertising medium. All economic incentives point to the intensification and extension of such practices.

The ability to cultivate children's time-slots, the core demand for children's programming that is relatively insensitive to program content, the attention-grabbing qualities of continuous action and violence, the ability to minimize costs by endless reruns and repackaged programming material, the greater vulnerability of children to advertising messages and their potential value to advertisers as in-house lobbyists—all are key characteristics of children's television that have yet to be fully exploited by the market. Specifically, how—and perhaps whether—they will be exploited depends significantly upon the position on the children's television issue ultimately adopted by the FCC.

5. Public Policy

It is somewhat ironic that public concern about children's television has intensified at a time when children have been specifically recognized as an audience justifying special treatment by broadcasters. Although parent groups have questioned children's television since the 1950s, during past periods the failure to recognize children as a special viewer group precluded such substantial response. In fact, current public response has been prompted by the special treatment of children as television viewers. This special treatment has not been based upon the needs or interests of children but on the effective exploitation of profitable markets. The outcry of public concern, likewise, has not been stimulated primarily by sudden awareness and concern for a positive plan to develop children's television based on the needs and interests of children. Indeed, these concerns have been pursued to a limited extent by activity outside commercial broadcasting in the public broadcasting sphere. The outcry is directed toward what great portions of the public consider to be abusive, exploitative, and harmful aspects of the existing special treatment of children by the commercial broadcasting system.

This chapter examines the development of children's television into a major issue for public policy. It recognizes that there have been many claims that commercial children's television is exploitative and harmful to children. It also recognizes that these claims, in turn, have been officially accepted by the FCC as having sufficient basis to warrant examination as a serious issue for public policy consideration. However, it makes no attempt to evaluate any specific claims against the programming and advertising policies and practices of the broadcast and network companies in children's television. What is important is that the claims have been recognized by the regulatory authority as having a substantial foundation. And what this study hopes to shed some light on is what one can expect in the future under possible alternative regulatory policies, including the alternative of doing nothing.

AROUSING A NATION OF PARENTS

The assassinations and social turmoil of 1968 again brought widespread public concern about the causes of such violence. The Eisenhower commission on "The Causes and Prevention of Violence" was established to study the problem. In 1969, the task-force report condemned "serious, non-comic" violent elements in children's shows. Although at the start of the 1969–70 season the networks replaced ten programs considered to be particularly violent and took steps to reduce violence on other children's shows, a study by Gerbner for the Surgeon General's report revealed that, although television violence declined in 1970 compared with 1969, children's cartoons were "still by far" the most violent of television programs.[1]

Further, the old objectionable programs were still being syndicated and broadcast by many stations around the country and the world, and therefore were being viewed by millions of children. In this respect, the syndication market functions much as a "used program" market for off-network reruns. It seems that most old filmed programs never die; they simply go into syndication. This has been particularly true for many UHF stations, which are marginal operations financially and are therefore primarily concerned with economic survival. In many broadcast markets, an independent (often UHF) station, has become the "children's station," showing endless reruns of old network programs.

There has also been a growing realization of the tremendous impact television has on the acculturation process of the young. Statistics on the amount of time children watch television compared with time spent in school or even sleeping, and the volumes of other research on the effects of the medium on children, increasingly demonstrate that television's overall impact on children is a topic that cannot be dismissed lightly. Although television is in many instances replacing the role of the traditional institutions such as schools, family, and church in children's lives, it has been relatively free of the legal and moral constraints that are imposed on the other institutions in their dealings with children.

Although some areas of programming service, such as news and public affairs, are differentiated from regular programming in that they are not expected to be highly profitable, virtually all commercial children's programming is designed and planned to yield broadcasters and networks maximum profit. Many complaints about children's television stem from the fact that the broadcast industry in general has not demonstrated by its actions—although it has by its rhetoric—that children deserve special consideration as part of the broader obligation to broadcast in the public interest. Broadcasters have apparently equated their public trusteeship responsibilities in the area of children's programming exactly with their commercial interest in maximizing profit, and complainants have thus concluded that such practices are violations of their public-interest responsibilities.

Objections to children's programming are directed at almost every dimension of programming policy and selection. For example, it is claimed that scheduling practices are not in the children's best interests, but are those most profitable for the broadcasters. On Saturday mornings, broadcasters are able to deliver to the advertisers a demographically pure audience at a lower CPM (cost per thousand) than is possible for a comparable audience at any other time. On weekday evenings, however, when adults as well as children will be watching, there is little programming specifically designed for children because it is more profitable to appeal to the broader audience spectrum, especially since children will be watching even if the programming is for adults. Complaints also address the lack of appropriate diversification, age specificity, and responsiveness to children's needs in children's programming.

The use of television advertising practices that take unfair advantage of children has been a major issue for some time. Increasingly, critics have begun to question whether children should be the subject of advertising messages at all. The reasons are varied: that they are psychologically unable to assess the value of product differences; that they lack the maturity of judgment to evaluate manufacturers' claims; that they are not the ones who must actually buy the product, and therefore to induce them to pressure their parents into a decision is not ethical; and, that the constant bombardment of commercials to acquire things induces materialism, frustration, and family friction, etc. Since only four or five product categories make up the bulk of the advertising to children, the problem has also been attacked in terms of the unsuitability of advertising each of these products to children. In 1970, for example, Robert B. Choate presented evidence to a consumer subcommittee of the Senate that cereal manufacturers were promoting the cereals with the least nutritional value to children.[2] In 1971 Action for Children's Television presented petitions to the FTC to prohibit vitamin and toy advertising to children.

Other issues of unreasonable practices of "commercialism" in children's television have also been raised. Children's programs during the daytime are allowed to have twice as much commercial time as evening programs, and twice as many program interruptions.[3] Advertising on children's programs has been so frequent that a serious problem of advertising "clutter" has been created for networks and advertisers. In addition, instances of hard-sell techniques to children have been called into question.

THE ACT PETITION AND FCC RECOGNITION

Early in 1970 the FCC took note of the problems with children's television when it decided to publish a petition for rule-making in this area, and opened up the whole matter for public comment. The catalyst in this action was an organization called Action for Children's Television (ACT), a group of citizens who had organized in response to the violent events of 1968, with a common concern about what was available to children on television.

According to ACT, the purpose of the petition for rule-making was "to substitute a new system of financial support of children's programming by commercial underwriting and public service funding in the belief that this system would look to the benefits of children rather than the profits of advertisers." By accepting the ACT petition, the FCC served notice to the broadcasting industry of its concern with children's television, and the possibility of regulatory policy determination in this area. Consideration of the ACT petition by the FCC is noteworthy in that it signaled an acknowledgment by the Commission of the mandates to action laid down in recent court decisions, and formally recognized the problems implied by the conflict of public and private interests in the area of children's television. The significance of the FCC's consideration of this petition transcends either the nature of the group that filed it or the contents of the petition itself. Until consideration of its petition was announced, ACT had enjoyed little more notoriety than a number of similarly motivated and constituted groups working toward improving television.

ACT had some notable successes in influencing local station decisions in 1968 and 1969, and had testified before governmental committees several times before submitting its petition to FCC. ACT appeared at the Pastore Committee hearings in the fall of 1969, before the FCC Cable Policy hearings, and in January 1970 at the FCC hearings on the Ascertainment of Community Needs by Broadcasters.

Since the ACT petition was accepted by the FCC, ACT has become the rallying point for those pursuing similar goals; but it should be emphasized that there was nothing about the institutional strength of the group that commanded FCC attention. The consideration of the petition showed recognition of the fundamental issues involved, not an acquiescence to institutional pressures.

In January 1971, the FCC published a Notice of

Proposed Rulemaking and Notice of Inquiry on the ACT proposal and asked for responses from interested parties.[4] The notice occasioned responses from major broadcast institutions, as well as more than 100,000 letters and supporting petitions from private citizens and citizen groups—the largest public response in the history of broadcast regulation. The overwhelming majority of the responses favored the ACT proposal. Also in 1971, the FCC established a Children's Television Unit and commissioned a study of "The Economics of Network Children's Television Programming," by FCC economist Alan Pearce.

The ACT petition included three major recommendations: (1) that no commercials be allowed on children's programs; (2) that performers and hosts of programs be forbidden to use or sell products by brand name during children's programs; and (3) that each station be required to provide a minimum of fourteen hours per week of children's programming, divided into age-specific groupings for preschool, primary, and elementary school age-groups.

In formally recognizing that many problems exist in children's television, the FCC elected, in its investigation, to go beyond the specific issues posed by the ACT petition and examine even more broadly and deeply the ramifications stemming from the existing institutional environment in which children's television is fully embraced as part of the commercial system. FCC chairman Burch recognized the core issue when he asked "whether a commercially-based broadcasting system is capable of serving up quality programming for an audience so sensitive and malleable as children."

The FCC also announced hearings for October 1972, at which the perspectives of a broad range of interested parties could be discussed before the Commission. Three days of panel discussion revolved around the principal issues surrounding children's television: content diversification, age specificity in programming, responsive scheduling, children's television and advertising practices, alternative methods of financing, and self-regulation. The format of the hearings indicated that the hearings used the ACT petition as a base for considering the broadest implications of children's television issues. As one would expect at such hearings, there was substantial disagreement among the participants on the panels and no easy solutions were forthcoming. The hearings were followed by three days of oral argument before the Commission in January 1973.

RESPONSE OF THE BROADCAST INDUSTRY

When the FCC issued its Notice of Proposed Rulemaking on Children's Television, the industry was faced with the real possibility of regulatory policy limiting its ability to realize profits on children's television. Broadcast management admitted its deficiencies and indicated that steps could, and would, be taken to correct them. Such claims, of course, were not new.

In 1960, FCC Chief of the Network Office, Ashbrook P. Bryant, observed that "there is almost uniform agreement—both within the industry and among public groups—that much needs to be done in the kind and quality of children's programs. During the session of our program inquiry in New York last year, many top creative professionals in television programming, as well as the representatives of some of the largest television advertisers, repeatedly identified children's programming as one of the principle deficiencies in network schedules." [5]

This renewed interest brought new elevated status to children's programming at the networks, with the creation by all three networks of directors of children's programming, but this was not unprecedented either. In 1962, during the "Minow-scare" phase, ABC had appointed a full-time director of children's programming.

One area in which broadcasters took action (although it had been recognized as a problem for some time) was deceptive advertising practices. In 1970 the National Association of Broadcasters (NAB) issued guidelines for toy commercials, one of the more objectionable perpetrators of misleading selling techniques directed at children. By the end of 1971 the issue of "overcommercialism" in children's television had also been considered through revised provisions in the NAB Television Code (effective January 1, 1973), reducing the amount of "non-program material in weekend children's programs" from sixteen to twelve minutes an hour, and the number of interruptions in these programs from eight to four. Children's program hosts or primary cartoon characters are also forbidden to deliver commercial messages during or adjacent to their own programs. To deal with the lack of "diversity" in children's programming, the networks and several group-owned stations introduced several "quality" programs in the 1970–71 season, with much pre-air publicity about the increased amounts of money, personnel, and lead time being committed to them. As best as can be determined, to a broadcaster a "quality" show is one in which costs are not minimized and profits are not maximized.

All of these actions, however, did little to change many of the objectionable practices that led to the FCC Notice. In regulating toy advertising, the broadcasters had only touched on the tip of an iceberg. On the question of vitamin advertising to children, for example, the NAB defended the practice on the grounds that flavored, chewable vitamins are foods, not drugs. A study, prepared for ACT by Earle Barcus, of Saturday morning programming from June 1971 to November 1971 in the Boston area, showed that the number of vitamin advertisements had significantly increased over the previous year. It was the vitamin manufacturers, rather than the broadcast industry, however, who finally yielded to the pressure of public dissatisfaction with the practice, when three of the major companies announced, in July 1972, that they would no longer use children's television programs to advertise their children's vitamin products. They concluded that such advertising was no longer in their own best interests.

The NAB Code revisions reducing commercial time in weekend children's programming were also a relatively minor change in light of the magnitude of the problem, which clearly reflected the primary influence of profit-making objectives. Evelyn Sarson pointed out that the NAB proposal:

> neglected to mention that this special protection still allows more selling to children than the eight to ten minutes in adult evening prime time programs. It also circumvents five-sevenths of the week when children are watching. . . . Furthermore, the Code Board is not planning to begin these minimal changes in September, when everyone knows the New Season begins. Instead, it postpones the move until January 1973, in order not to lose the profitable pre-Christmas trade.[6]

The programming changes initiated by the networks and a few stations also did little to alleviate the problems of homogeneous programming and nonoptimal scheduling practices. Of approximately eighteen hours of children's programming on Saturday morning on the three networks in September 1971, only four and a half were the much publicized "quality" shows, and three of these programs were scheduled competitively, on Saturday afternoon, when children's viewing drops off considerably.[7] In 1962, when the networks also undertook a much publicized attempt to upgrade their children's programming, Jack Gould observed that these otherwise meritorious programming attempts were self-defeated by traditional scheduling and advertising practices[8]—a situation that events in 1971 seemed to parallel closely.

A serious problem with any attempts to improve children's television programming at the network level is that, although the stations often allow the networks to assume their programming responsibilities largely by default, they most often do this when it is also *profitable* for them to do so. A major reason that quality network shows have failed over the years has been the unwillingness of stations to clear them. In other words, if the stations have more profitable opportunities for selling their time-slots to advertisers, they may not choose to follow the lead of the networks in supplying some "quality" programming that does not maximize profits.

THE PEARCE STUDY

In July 1972, the FCC released the study on "The Economics of Network Children's Television" conducted by Alan Pearce. The purposes of the Pearce study were: (1) to give a brief outline of the main economic characteristic of broadcast advertising, i.e. the greater the audience tuned into a program, the lower the costs per viewer; (2) to list the major advertisers in children's programming and the extent of their financial support of network children's programs; (3) to outline the costs and revenues of children's programming; (4) to explore the financial impact on the networks of a reduction of commercial time in children's weekend programming; and (5) to examine the broad economic implications to the networks of the ACT petition on children's programming.

Release of the Pearce study was immediately followed by assertions on the part of the various commercial interests in the children's television controversy that it supported their claims. The advertising industry noted that implementation of the ACT proposal would cut network revenues by almost $56 million and require higher prices on other programs. *Variety* concluded that children's television is highly profitable and might easily absorb the effects of a 25 percent reduction in commercial time. In short, the more significant contributions of the Pearce study were not emphasized.

The study revealed the enormously high degree of concentration in the advertising market for children's programs. The three leading advertisers in network weekend children's television—Kellogg, Mattel, and General Mills—account for approximately 30 percent of the total revenues from children's shows. The top eight advertisers account for about 55 percent of revenues, and the top twenty-three advertisers account for 80 percent of gross revenues. Moreover, the concentration by product was revealed to be extremely high too, with cereal manufacturers, toy manufacturers, vitamins and non-prescription drugs, and food, candy, and beverages dominating the market. This data clearly shows how network weekend children's television has become a specialized commercial market for a specialized group of advertisers, with advertising messages uniquely adapted to the children's audience.

The Pearce study also explored in some detail the costs and revenues of networks' children's programming, concluding that the costs of the cartoon fare that constitutes most of children's weekend television is between $10,000 and $11,000 per half-hour on the average, based upon an assumption of six showings over a two-year period. However, these costs do not take into account the additional market potential for syndication after the two-year period. In contrast, Pearce found programming costs of about $250,000 per hour for first showings of network prime-time children's television. Revenues, of course, varied according to individual program and network, depending upon particular circumstances.

The study explored in some detail the pricing and revenue structures of the children's television market, breaking the analysis down by network, time of presentation, and individual program. It went on to calculate net profit effects based upon certain assumptions concerning the effect of gross revenue reductions implied by cutting back commercial minutes. Pearce noted that a 25 percent reduction in commercial content would reduce CBS' revenues by $6.3 million but would still provide a profit contribution of $10 million from children's television. NBC's profitability from children's programming would be reduced from $3.7 million to $1 million; ABC's would be reduced from $7.2 million to $3.5 million.

Interpretation of these calculations requires a thorough understanding of their assumptions. The Pearce study notes:

Throughout the computations above, an unrealistic assumption has been made—that is, that price per minute would remain the same if the amount of commercial content in children's programming were reduced. As we have seen, relatively few advertisers account for most of the advertising revenue derived from children's programming, and these advertisers have a fairly inelastic—that is a reasonably fixed—demand for the available commercial positions in children's programming. . . . Consequently, in an oligopolistic situation where relatively few advertisers are competing for time offered by three suppliers, prices will increase if a situation of scarcity is created.[9]

Hence, it is apparent that the calculations are based upon a set of assumptions that are theoretically designed to test the worst possible case in terms of impact upon the profitability of the networks. They therefore provide an evaluation of the absolute minimum base level of change that could take place without threatening the substantial profitability of the networks' broadcasting operations. The tasks that remain before a decision can be reached on the financial aspects of children's television, require extension of the analysis to consider the consequences of specific proposed changes.

Finally, Pearce examined the ACT proposal within the framework of the model that he used to make the calculations of potential profit reductions to the networks. Assuming that advertising prices would remain the same despite the newly created scarcity, that other sources of revenues—institutional ads, underwriting, or government support—would not be forthcoming in any significant amount, and that existing commercial broadcast institutions would continue to plan and produce programs in the current manner, Pearce concluded that the proposal would result in a serious financial loss to all three networks. The study also examined the feasibility of a plan for age-specific programming, and concluded that if properly structured so that the three networks shared the burden of those areas of age-specific programming which would be unprofitable, it would not be unfeasible to attempt such a restructuring of the children's market. However, it is important to recognize that the Pearce study "concentrated on analyzing the situation as it exists, or as it is seen to exist in the minds of network executives." It did not consider changes in the existing broadcast structure for children's programming. Nevertheless, it does provide the basis for further analysis of alternatives and for estimates of their consequences.

With the Pearce study, the FCC hearings and oral argument, and the broadcast industry's response, our review and analysis of the development of the public-policy issue in children's programming is brought up to date. The FCC is presently deliberating on the issue and planning subsequent steps. In a later chapter, we shall consider the range of policy options open to it and the potential consequences of each. But first, we shall examine the scope and limitations of the FCC's power to develop policy in commercial children's television.

6.   Public Policy: The Past*

Issues affecting the public's interests in television broadcasting must ultimately be assessed in light of the
regulatory responsibilities of the FCC and the public-policy options available to it. The problems relating to
children's television have been recognized by the FCC as
matters for policy consideration, but there are questions
as to the specific responsibilities of the Commission, the
limits of its authority, and the range of alternative policy
options that could be adopted by it. This chapter reviews
and assesses the role of regulation by the FCC as it might
be brought to bear on the children's television issues.

The market structure of the television broadcast
industry does not represent the evolution of free market
forces. Rather, that structure reflects, to a major degree,
the application by the FCC of public policy determined
by government regulation. Television broadcasting was
recognized at its inception as "business affected with a
public interest," and thus possessing particular rights and
obligations.

This unique relationship between broadcasters and
regulatory authority has been determined principally by
the technology of broadcasting. Broadcasting requires the
use of a scarce and valuable public resource, the
electromagnetic spectrum, to supply its over-the-air service. Thus, there cannot be freedom of entry to broadcast

* With Douglas Richardson

markets. Entry is regulated through the FCC's licensing process, which together with the Commission's other regulatory policies, determines the structure of broadcast markets.

The scarcity of broadcast channels and the FCC's requirements for the licensing of broadcast stations severely restrict the force of competition in broadcast markets, thus creating significant concentrations of economic power and private control over the content of television and the terms and conditions of access to broadcast markets. But when a broadcaster is granted and accepts the free and exclusive use of this scarce and valuable public resource, he also accepts public obligations. The public broadcast channel can only be used under the terms and conditions of the license. And one who accepts use of a publicly owned broadcast channel becomes a "trustee" for the public. In instances of conflict between the public interest and the broadcaster's own commercial interests, the public interest must take precedence. The continuance of a license depends upon evaluation by the FCC of the performance of the broadcaster in discharging his responsibility to the public.

THE DELEGATION OF AUTHORITY TO THE FCC

Any legislative or quasi-legislative activity derives its legitimacy, and ultimately its practical efficacy, from some original delegation of power and from some mandate concerning how that power can be used. In the case of the FCC, that mandate came from the U.S. Congress in the Communications Act of 1934,[1] which delegated to the Commission the authority to regulate the relationship between a system of broadcasting that uses private licensees who have the responsibility for selecting and presenting programming, and the interests of the general public, which theoretically retains net control of the channels over which the programming is broadcast.

To enable it to discharge its role as trustee for the public interest, Congress granted the FCC broad discretionary powers, powers circumscribed by relatively few specifically articulated guidelines. The 1934 Act clearly indicated a congressional desire to have the FCC accept responsibility for developing the specific standards of broadcast regulation and policy-making. In doing so, the Congress acknowledged its own relative lack of expertise with respect to communications and a confidence that the FCC would act affirmatively to solve the immediate problems prompting congressional action, and to build a satisfactory body of law upon which broadcasters could base their activity.

It must be noted that the Federal Communications Act of 1934, which was a sequel to the 1927 Radio Act, was hurriedly written and passed by Congress in response to immediate and sharply perceived structural needs: the years preceding the act had been marked by increasing confusion in the broadcast industry concerning wavelength allocations, signal interference, power, locations, and other technical problems that threatened to drown the potential of the new medium in incoherence and internecine warfare.

What occurred, therefore, was the phenomenon of a new industry coming to the government and asking that it be regulated—a phenomenon that assured the industry an active role in determining the form that regulation would take. The 1934 act reflected an immediate concern for establishing a stable industry rather than any visionary consideration of what patterns might emerge in the long run, after these initial structures were firmly established. Because of this original preoccupation with the technical aspects of broadcast regulation, basic policy considerations were couched in terminology so broad that they offered few real standards or guidelines for broadcaster behavior.

Yet it was the conditions of technical regulation that required restrictions on entry into broadcasting via licensing, the creation of concentrations of economic power, and the control over access and content by private broadcast interests. It is these latter problems that have proven to be those of greatest public import and concern since the passage of the Communications Act.

Consonant with its constitutional right to delegate such power to agencies and commissions as might enable them to operate in the "public interest, convenience, and necessity," Congress vested in the FCC the authority not only to oversee the technical aspects of licensing, but also to monitor industry behavior and perform quasi-judicial and quasi-legislative functions—that is, to hold hearings and make rules. Although Section 326 of the 1934 Act prohibits the FCC from censoring program content— content being the responsibility of the broadcaster—subsequent court decisions have given the Commission considerable latitude in overseeing general areas of program content and industry behavior—all with respect to serving the public interest.[2]

After establishing this affirmative responsibility with the broadcasters and the FCC to regulate the discharge of that responsibility, Congress thereupon effectively withdrew from the arena. For the most part, Congress has indicated that it has no desire to reassume direct legislative responsibility for assuring the balance of interests between the private licensee and the public at large; although frequently criticized on the floor of Congress, the 1934 act has remained largely unchanged over the years, and overseeing of the FCC's function has come, most significantly, from the courts.[3]

LIMITS ON THE REGULATORY PROCESS

A number of external factors have come to impinge on the manner in which the FCC perceives and discharges its regulatory function. Among these is the fact that broadcast networks, which have become enormously powerful institutions, can be regulated only indirectly by the FCC. Because the networks do not themselves use the air waves, but rather organize markets and distribute a "product" to affiliated stations for broadcast, they do not fall within the scope of the 1934 Act and can be regulated only by constraints put upon the affiliates with whom they deal. Such was the case, for example, in 1941, when licensees were made subject to chain broadcasting regulations intended to further competition in broadcasting by placing limits on concentration of media ownership. And more recently (1970), the FCC adopted its "Prime Time Access" rule in an attempt to diversify sources of television programming from existing levels of network concentration.

Moreover, from the outset the FCC has faced the problem of administering policy in a number of different areas—common carrier regulation, radio regulation, television regulation[4]—with both a relatively limited staff and relatively limited funding. With respect to television, the scarcity of these resources has affected the Commission's ability to move aggressively on all regulatory fronts; priorities have been set to ensure stability and continuity within the Commission.

The role of the broadcasting industry in initiating regulation and determining the form that regulation will take, has been noted. A comparatively high industry profile exists to this day; if unable to impinge directly on FCC decision-making, the industry nonetheless has long possessed high-powered tools to enunciate and clarify its wants and interests. The 1952 McFarland amendments to the 1934 Act were designed to prevent direct, ex parte leverage on the Commission, but even their presence could not alter the relative resource strengths of the regulator and the regulated; by virtue of the sheer magnitude of its vested interests, the broadcasting industry has played a powerful role in the regulatory environment.

The relative scarcity of FCC resources and manpower has also acted to inhibit the aggressiveness of Commission action. Monitoring functions could not be as thorough as desired; industry performance and compliance with regulatory law had to be carried out largely on the honor system, and the Commission usually awaited initiation of a complaint from other quarters before taking action. In addition, priorities had to be set in which long-range planning functions were subordinated to day-to-day administrative procedures. Policy therefore came to be formulated on an ad hoc, case-by-case basis, rather than on long-range policy goals and programs of action.

Whether because of lack of insulation from industry sources or limited resources, until the time of recent court decisions, the FCC has assumed a deliberately passive regulatory stance. The decision clearly was made that the broadcast licensees would be assigned an affirmative role in insuring fairness, while the FCC stood in the background as field umpire. To this end, the Commission spoke, for example, of a licensee's "affirmative duty

generally to encourage and implement broadcast of all
sides of controversial public issues," while describing its
own role far less aggressively:

> In passing on any complaint, the Commission's role is
> not to substitute its judgment for that of the licensee
> . . . but rather to determine whether the licensee can
> be said to have acted reasonably and in good faith.
> . . . The Commission has never laid down, and does
> not now propose to lay down, any categorical answers.
> . . . Rather than enunciating general policies, the
> Commission reaches decisions on matters in the cruci-
> ble of particular cases.[5]

This determination to develop a body of regulatory
law and policy on a case-by-case basis has frequently
been attacked as failing to provide coherence and
continuity to regulatory policy and as setting up guidelines so vague that they represent no real standards by
which the industry can measure its own behavior.

It has been suggested that this passive approach to
regulation indicated recognition by the Commission that
it lacked the capability to implement and administer
rigorously defined guidelines: the Commission's tendency
to act instead as a consensus-finder among competing
interests, has been seen by some as a function both of the
conditions under which it was born and the environment
in which it must operate.[6]

Red Lion, THE PEOPLE, AND THE "DOUBLE AFFIRMATIVE"

Despite floods of law review rhetoric and periodic bills
introduced to reorganize and restructure the FCC, the
Commission continued to show an aversion to rule-

making and formulation of standards until quite recently. Although vested with the power to set standards and policy guidelines in both technical and nontechnical areas, the FCC used its rule-making abilities only when confronted with an urgent situation requiring immediate resolution, such as the controversy surrounding appearances of political candidates on television.

Similarly, the Commission has long been hesitant to exercise the sanctions authorized by the congressional delegation of power. The one real regulatory weapon of the Commission, revocation of license, was apparently so odious a punishment, involving as it did total exclusion from the economic market, that it was seldom used. Instead, the FCC made frequent use of "the raised eyebrow," a technique that indicated Commission displeasure to the licensee without implying immediate economic disaster. Once again, these gentle slaps on the wrist were consonant with the "actively passive" role the Commission had assumed, and with its recognition of its limited ability to enforce sanctions.

In 1969 the Supreme Court forced a wholesale change in the Commission's orientation toward its duties, in the now famous *Red Lion* case.[7] In that case, the Court espoused a "double affirmative" responsibility of broadcast regulation, particularly in the policy-making areas. The Court said, in effect, that the *FCC* had an affirmative duty to make certain that the *broadcasters* acted affirmatively to program in the public interest. In earlier cases, notably the 1942 *NBC* case,[8] the courts had granted the Commission extensive powers to control general areas of content and policy; in the *Red Lion* case, the Court demanded that the FCC exercise that authority. The element of discretion that had underpinned the Commission's ability to act passively had been removed.

The decision of the Supreme Court to impinge upon the FCC's autonomy followed several developments that forced the Commission into a more active stance with respect to program policy. Judicial review of FCC decisions was placing FCC performance under more rigorous standards of accountability, and in the landmark *WLBT* case[9] it found abuse of discretionary power and ultimately reversed an FCC decision. The rise of public-interest groups brought challenges to the renewal of broadcast licenses for failure to program or operate in the public interest, and promoted exploration into ways to affect the interface between the FCC and the broadcast industry. These developments brought increased visibility to the practices, of both the commission and the broadcasting industry. *Red Lion*, therefore, not only forced the FCC into action, but encouraged public participation in initiating proceedings to assure accountability of the FCC to the public and of licensees to the FCC.

THE NEW ACCOUNTABILITY

The FCC, as a result of new and compelling pressures, *cannot* decline to make decisions in important policy areas. Whatever its lack of resources, whatever its present lack of enforcement machinery, whatever its present limitations in terms of long-range planning, the authority to act in economic and policy areas has evolved into a mandate to act in these areas. The underlying power of the FCC has not changed, nor has the countervailing power of the industry whose behavior the Commission was created to regulate. What *has* changed are the standards of accountability; increased visibility to the public, and firm demands coming from the courts for affirmative Commission action, mean that the FCC has little choice but to assume a more active role, in terms of rule-making, policy-making, planning, and implementing its decisions.

Now, even in the face of resource shortage, the FCC has been told it must assume affirmative responsibility for the behavior of broadcast licensees or return to court time and again to explain why it is failing to meet the stiffer standards of accountability. The end result, combining the original congressional mandate and recent pressures to action, is a commission empowered to regulate technical, economic, and certain public-interest aspects of broadcasting, and now required to act positively to employ that regulatory power.

THE SCOPE OF PERMISSIBLE REGULATION

Though the powers delegated to the FCC by Congress in the 1934 act are extremely broad, there has been continuing controversy concerning the proper subjects for FCC regulation and the permissible scope of that regulation. Throughout this controversy, the broadcast industry has periodically appeared to argue both sides of the basic substantive issues surrounding Commission activity. While using first amendment and Section 326 (the 1934 act's anticensorship provision) to argue that Commission activity in economic and general program content areas exceeds both constitutional authority and authority delegated to the Commission by Congress, the broadcasters simultaneously assert that the FCC's ad hoc approach to policy-making prevents them from forming a stable set of expectations upon which they can act and predict government response.

As has been noted above, the first of these positions

received a mortal blow at the hands of the Supreme Court in the *Red Lion* case. Not only did the court reaffirm the initial delegation of authority to the FCC and the earlier *NBC* decision granting the Commission broad latitude in the use of those powers in the public interest, but it also demanded that the Commission act affirmatively in overseeing those areas of broadcasting which affect the public, including economic and program-content aspects.

In the face of this denial of broadcasters' pleas for less accountability in terms of program-content decisions, the networks and broadcasters have retreated to the point where they are working to keep regulatory guidelines at present vague levels. ABC, for example, now asserts that "what is needed is not standards for day-to-day application by individual stations, but a broader determination of what constitutes [broadcast] fairness." Similarly, CBS and NBC have argued against the notion that the *Red Lion* decision created in the FCC an affirmative obligation to codify more stringent standards. NBC has claimed that regulation of content should be kept to "a broad general principle," and CBS has asserted that the *Red Lion* case did not "provide a mandate for making new rules."

Underlying these points of view is the broadcasters' notion that the broadcasting industry is no different in kind from other information-disseminating media, and that it should be regulated only with respect to those technical aspects of licensing, wavelength allocation, and broadcast power which reflect directly on the institutional stability of the industry. This position has not found currency either in the courts or among those determining policy. Comments such as these of former FCC commissioner Lee Loevinger are typical:

Although the FCC is not entitled to condition the grant, denial, or revocation of a broadcast license upon its own subjective determination of what is or is not a good program, since a broadcaster is regulated to program in the public interest, it follows, despite limitations of the first amendment and Section 326 of the Act that his freedom to program is not absolute.[10]

The FCC and the courts have consistently taken the position that the broadcast media are indeed unique in that the medium of distribution, i.e. the airwaves, is a valuable public resource; that broadcasting is a business affected with a public interest; that as a medium it is uniquely influential; and that there is relative scarcity of access to broadcast markets and to the use of channels.

Not only have broadcasters' arguments of nonuniqueness not prevailed, but it has even been suggested that the broadcasters are fortunate that their arguments have not prevailed. Roscoe Barrow notes that:

When government licenses the few to use the channels and forbids the many to interfere, it does so because there is a public interest to be served. . . . If the industry succeeds in striking down parts of FCC regulation as violations of the first amendment, it will be self-defeating because if there is no public interest to be served, there is no reason for government to protect broadcasters from the sharp competition which they have contended prevents them from serving the public interest.[11]

The absence of precise standards with which broadcasters would have to comply on economic and programming issues is consistent with the FCC's initial role as a monitor rather than a leader. The affirmative responsibility for programming in the public interest had originally been placed upon the broadcasters, and in a developmental era in which both regulators and regulatees were pioneering in unfamiliar territory, it made some sense to cast the responsibility for defining the public interest upon the consciences of the broadcasters—subject, of course, to overview by the FCC. Functionally, precise codification or explication of the public-interest standard was seen as working against the industry's best interests. Such a definition or set of definitions would circumscribe broadcaster flexibility with respect to content, and possibly force him to adopt programming that conflicted with the efficiency and profitability of his business.

For its part, the Commission was no more eager to spell out the details of phrases that floated at a high moral level of abstraction; to do so would have been to impose upon itself the onus of enforcing what could be an incredibly demanding system of monitoring, evaluation, complaint origination, and adjudication. Inability to implement its own standards could not help the Commission's prestige, and proper administration of detailed standards of behavior would force it to abandon its passive role.

Yet there was a need to develop some objective indication by which satisfaction of public-interest requirements might be measured. The broadcasters chose a form that neither impaired their programming flexibility nor deprived them of figures upon which they could evaluate the costs of fulfilling the public-interest requirement. License renewal applications became vehicles by which stations could assess and chronicle: (1) the amount of public-interest advertising spots—at a cost that could be determined; (2) the amount of sustaining (nonsponsored) programming—assumed to be public interest because public-interest programs are unpopular with sponsors; (3) the amount of news programming—usually a loss leader; and (4) the amount of childrens' programming—its mere presence somehow carrying the presumption that it was in the children's interest.

Because of the recent petition by ACT presently before the FCC, we may soon see a decision concerning the extent to which the broadcasters' affirmative duty to program in the public interest will be allowed to impinge upon broadcasters' commercial operations. The petition requests termination of all commercial advertising on programming geared for children and an allotment of a minimum of fourteen hours a week for childrens' programming.

The question of defining justifiable areas of public interest has been made an issue here, for the ACT petition depends upon the notion that children are an identifiable group with unique rights, requiring treatment different from that accorded other audiences. That ACT does not demand changes in other sectors of commercial broadcasting underscores this dichotomy. The idea of a special public interest in children becomes salient because of the purported economic ramifications of the ACT petition. If, as ACT contends, the idea of acting in the public interest requires more than merely putting on programs that won't tangibly hurt children, then it is entirely possible that constructive efforts in that direction will entail economic costs not existing under present arrangements.

Although the broadcasters argue that children are not a unique audience—just as they earlier argued that broadcasting is not a unique medium—the fact that they schedule their childrens' programming in one time area—Saturday and Sunday mornings for the most part—and the fact that they create program and advertisement formats that are unique to the child audience, indicate that they do conceive of the child audience as unique, at least as a market for advertising purposes.

Upcoming FCC decisions concerning children's programming will undoubtedly say a great deal about whether the public-interest standard becomes a concrete index of broadcaster accountability, or remains a formula for determining minimum compliance at license-renewal time. The critical question becomes whether or not the uniqueness of the child audience is of a sort which the FCC must force broadcasters to respect as a function of their affirmative public-interest responsibility. It is argued that, because of their extreme impressionability and lack of discrimination, children are inappropriate targets for commercial merchandising practices, and, therefore, high-powered attempts to influence their tastes for food and toys run contrary to the public interest.

Analogies from other areas of law concerning the rights of children support the notion that they are entitled to greater protection and insulation from commercial influence than is the case with other segments of the population. The underlying policy behind our history of special legal protection is to prevent children from damaging themselves by their own improvident acts and from being victims of the deception of others. Child labor laws, for example, were enacted to prevent the young from being exploited as cheap labor in sweatshops or other dangerous occupations.

Contracts made by children have long been held to be voidable, i.e. terminable at the will of the child making the contract; this merely represents the admission of policy- and lawmakers that children are not knowledge-able in business areas, and are uniquely susceptible to practices and pressures used in the business community. A New York court, for example, held in the case of *Bookcase, Inc.* v. *Broderick*,[12] that a statute was not unconsti-tutional which prohibited the sale to minors of matter which is not obscene in the hands of adults. The court said: "The Plaintiff's constitutional right to make a profit may not take precedence over the legitimate and exigent power of the state to protect the welfare of its youth" (267 NYS 2nd at 418). Similarly, the Supreme Court has reached much the same conclusion with respect to the policies surrounding dealings with the young. In *Prince* v. *Massachusetts*,[13] the Supreme Court held that concern for children's welfare could justify limitations on even the most sacred of American freedoms: "The state's authority over children's activities is broader than over like actions of adults." [14]

In the law of torts, there have been such protective doctrines as that of attractive nuisance, which, for example, puts duties on landowners that would not exist if the person in jeopardy were adult; the child, ostensibly, cannot appreciate, understand, or avoid the nature of the danger or hazard to which he is exposed, a notion which many contend applies to modern merchandising tactics as well. In *King* v. *Lennon*,[15] for example, the court held that even so obvious a danger as drowning in a swimming pool falls within the scope of the doctrine when the child is too young to understand the danger involved.

It has often been contended that, in an era when there is the possibility that television content is actually harmful to the healthy development of the child's psyche, it is the parent's responsibility to ensure that objectionable programming is filtered from the child's view. Yet a foremost authority in tort law, William L. Prosser, has said:

> While it is true that his parents or guardians are charged with the duty of looking after [the child], it is obviously neither customary nor practicable for them to follow him around with a keeper, or chain him to the bedpost. . . . Added to this is the traditional social interest in the safety and welfare of children.[16]

Obviously, parents have a moral duty to oversee their children's behavior and to shield them from influences which are, in the parent's judgment, potentially harmful. Since, however, the 1934 Communications Act placed a legal responsibility upon broadcasters to program for the best interests of the child audience, one can wonder why the need exists today for a parent to have to act as a shield. Were the networks and broadcasters fulfilling their responsibilities conscientiously, one might ask why the parental responsibility is not to select the *most desirable* alternatives offered to children, rather than to have to make the choice simply of leaving the television set on or turning it off. It is by recognizing children as a legitimate public-interest category that the courts have specifically extended the responsibilities set out in the 1934 Act to cover programming done especially for children.

This recognition by the courts may occasion a major affirmative policy action by the FCC in accordance with the judicial directive of the *Red Lion* decision, cited above. The Commission unquestionably has authority to act in areas affected with a public interest, and it has been told that it has an affirmative duty to act in these areas. It can no longer remain passive: if the area of children's programming and merchandising is held to embrace public-interest issues—as the above cases suggest—it follows that some action by the FCC must be forthcoming. The fact that such action may well have economic ramifications for the broadcasting industry is no longer valid justification for Commission inaction. The courts have demanded a more assertive attempt to balance the interests of the industry and the public it ostensibly serves—particularly the uniquely vulnerable subgroup of children viewers. Reluctance by the FCC to assume this responsibility will apparently result only in continuing and stronger mandates to action.

7.   Public Policy: The Future

The foregoing analysis has pointed up how the differences in primary objectives between the economic criteria of profit and the social criteria of children's needs and desires has created a fundamental conflict of priorities across the entire structure of the broadcast industry, its institutions, and their operations. As "public trustees," broadcasters are charged with performing in the public interest. According to regulatory law, the public interest takes precedence over the broadcaster's private economic interests: "it is the right of viewers and listeners, not the right of broadcasters, which is paramount."

Although this principle is clear in theory, in application the broadcaster must make a continuing series of trade-offs between his own private economic interests and the public's interests, as he interprets those interests. It is hardly surprising that he almost universally inverts the order of priorities between private and public interests. Indeed, that is why the FCC was created. Supposedly unencumbered by the constraints of a vested personal financial interest, the Commission is charged with the responsibility of ensuring that the trade-offs made between the public and private interests are socially beneficial.

Until the present time, in the area of children's television, the trade-offs between the public interest and private financial interests have been left to the industry. The analysis of earlier chapters has shown that, within

116

the industry, the fundamental decision-makers for these crucial trade-offs have not been the broadcast stations, which are under direct regulation by the FCC, but the broadcast networks, which do not have the same public-interest responsibilities imposed on them that are imposed on the stations. Thus, in these areas of decision-making the broadcast stations are not masters of their own fate. The real center of power for managerial discretion lies with the networks—institutions that do not have the formal legal obligations of public trusteeship. Trade-offs between public and private interests by broadcast stations in children's television become ancillary to those made by the networks.

The record of performance in children's television by the networks indicates that they have not treated children's television as a unique public-interest responsibility requiring them to deviate from their profit-maximizing behavior. This is so even though the networks have substantial monopoly power over both programming- and broadcast-station relations—power which in other industries occasions close government scrutiny via the antitrust laws and/or direct regulation. Similarly, the great majority of broadcast stations, although severely limited in their options by the overshadowing presence of network policies and practices, have not recognized children's television as a particular public-interest responsibility requiring deviation from their profit objectives.

In contrast, the ACT petition to the FCC requests a complete reversal of policy priorities, establishing the criterion of the needs and interests of children as the controlling purpose of children's television. The petition claims that the economic interests of the broadcast industry diverge substantially from what is in the interest of the child viewer, and concludes that the latter can never be appropriately served as long as children's television is being supplied in response to an advertiser-supported market. The FCC must now consider the scope of its regulatory discretion in determining an appropriate public-policy response on the issue.

CHILDREN'S TELEVISION AS AN ISSUE

There are two quite distinct aspects of the children's television issue. The first involves the problem of potential harm to children from such things as aggressive advertising techniques directed at them, and children's programs that reflect undesirable practices and consequences, e.g. violence. The second aspect addresses the positive side of the issue by examining the responsibilities for developing constructive children's programming in accordance with *only* their needs and interests. But even this distinction does not fully clarify the specific dimensions of the children's television issue before the FCC.

The question of protection from harm is not that children should be shielded from exposure to any and all advertising on television. Clearly, children always have and always will be exposed to advertising. The issue is whether children should be protected from being isolated as a specialized audience for the specific purpose of applying pinpoint and tailor-made advertising directed toward their particular vulnerabilities as children. The point to be considered is not whether children should be permitted to observe and grow up in the television-advertising game as played by adults. Rather, the question is, should children be protected from being singled out as the most vulnerable and malleable target for direct attack by television advertisers?

Similarly, it should be clear that the focus of concern is upon children, not on the advertisers of children's products. The protection of children from direct advertising would require that advertisers on children's programs merely modify their advertising plans. It would not deny them the opportunity to advertise elsewhere, as do many producers of children's products.

As for the programming aspect of children's television, the issue is not simply that there be some planned programming based solely on the needs and interests of children. We have already gone around commercial television to obtain some such services on public television. Indeed, the differences between children's television on public and commercial television are primarily attributable to the objectives of children's television on each system. Such programs as *Sesame Street*, *The Electric Company, Mr. Rogers,* and other programs, reflecting the activity of Children's Television Workshop and other producing units, are all directed toward the single objective of enriching the lives of the child viewer. This does not make them perfect. They make mistakes and are criticized for the way they go about trying to achieve their objectives, but the objectives are clear. Hence, it should not be surprising at all that public television, which is directed to the interests of children, has produced better programs than commercial children's television, which is directed to the interests of advertisers. However, since commercial television has an enormous command over and access to the nation's viewing audiences, far exceeding that of public television, the point for consideration is whether the special public responsibilities of the commercial broadcasters, which are a condition to their licensing by the FCC, warrant the development and implementation of a program of children's television designed to meet the needs and interests of children.

The special treatment of children has been clearly recognized by the law since time immemorial, and recently by the television networks and the advertising industry. In a press release describing its fall 1972 season offerings for children, CBS stated: "Children. They are our most precious resource. When they are entertained creatively and instructed with great care and imagination, all of society benefits." The Association of National Advertisers (ANA), in formulating guidelines for commercials on television aimed at children, said it recognized that children are a special group of viewers and that television plays an important role in their development. The guidelines, adopted by the ANA on July 6, 1972, are based on principles the advertisers' organization considers mandatory in communicating with children.

The pronouncements, of course, follow on the heels of the FCC Notice of Inquiry and Notice of Proposed Rulemaking, which stated, on this point:

> there are high public interest considerations involved in the use of television . . . in relation to a large and important segment of the audience, the Nation's children. The importance of this portion of the audience, and the character of material reaching it, are particularly great because its ideas and concepts are largely not yet crystallized and are therefore open to suggestion, and also because its members do not yet have the experience and judgment always to distinguish the real from the fanciful.[1]

Recognizing that children require special public-interest consideration, it becomes apparent that they need protection from being singled out as a market and specifically manipulated for the financial benefit of advertisers and broadcasters. Most of the claimed abuses have arisen precisely because the industry has become increasingly efficient at specializing in children's programming and advertising. The segmentation of the child audience was created to permit a more direct exploitation of the vulnerability of children. Thus, one cannot view the creation of new approaches, such as age-specific programming, as necessarily beneficial to children. If classifications are based upon considerations of profit and market exploitation, as they usually are, one can almost certainly expect abuses to appear. In fact, the segregation of children's markets for exploitation by advertisers may be much worse than having no children's programming classifications at all.

The positive side of the issue recognizes that there is a responsibility to create classifications of children's programming on the basis of the needs and interest of children. That such classifications should be used on the commercial broadcast system as opposed to the public system recognizes that public broadcasting cannot fully meet the special needs of children. It also recognizes that the commercial system has much broader exposure to the general public and that vast numbers of children will be watching commercial broadcasting anyway. Most of the nation has access to the commercial broadcast system and is well used to viewing the commercial channels, while only limited numbers of the population have access to the public broadcast system. Moreover, the commercial broadcaster has definite public-service responsibilities that he cannot ignore or leave for public broadcasting to assume.

The issue of children's television, then, boils down to:

(1) ensuring that children are not singled out on the basis of advertising market criteria for pinpoint exploitation by advertisers; and (2) ensuring that children are singled out for special programming on the basis of their own needs and interests. This, in turn, raises the crucial question: can these objectives really be met within the framework of an advertiser-based, commercial broadcast system?

A FORECAST

Although children's television is currently an issue high on the public agenda, one is naturally led to question the permanence both of awareness of the problem and the persistence of the public that is taking active interest. Now that the issues have been exposed, can we expect some self-correction within the next few years? Can we expect industry to realize that it must modify its private financial interests somewhat and place children's television higher up on its public-interest list of priorities?

The nature of market development within the broadcasting industry would indicate that the trend toward specialization in children's programming, as well as other demographically determined, specialized classifications, will not only continue but will also become much more sophisticated. Indeed, this is the way the market system is supposed to work. As the total market grows, it becomes economical and profitable to begin creating specialized market classifications that can be tailored more closely to the requirements of each classification of customers. Children's audiences represent a classification that enables particular kinds of advertisers to get direct access to the audience without having to go through the filter of a larger mass audience.

Television broadcasting is just now entering a phase of market development that will lead to substantially increased market specialization. In children's programming, this means the programs and advertisements will be more effective in exploiting the vulnerabilities of children in pinpoint fashion. Consequently, more complaints against its harmful effects can be expected. The greater the degree of market and submarket specialization in children's television, the greater the exploitation of children, and the more serious public concern will tend to be. If the public interest is identified with the prevention of pinpoint advertiser exploitation of children, then the continued pursuit of specialization of children's markets will be directly contrary to the public interest under the existing industry structure and regulation. Content diversification and age specificity, both important to children's interest groups, will be created, but the purpose will be to permit market exploitation. The children's classifications will be based upon the advertisers' interests rather than the child's.

Moreover, the economic realities of this trend make it unlikely that it will be easily modified by good intentions or self-regulation. The specialization era in children's television is just beginning and has already had an enormous payoff. The latest and most sophisticated information-gathering and analytical techniques are already being employed for the purpose of identifying new, potentially profitable markets. There is substantial evidence that continuing market segmentation has a great future in children's television.

The substantial profitability from such specialization virtually guarantees that the broadcast industry will follow this path. As time passes, the financial sacrifice that would accompany any decision to forego the specialization alternative will continue to increase, thus making it virtually inevitable that the broadcasters will pursue this line of development.

If the FCC elects to take no action on the children's television issues before it now, it appears inevitable that the presently operative economic forces in the industry will work to make the problems more serious, and intensify criticisms and concerns that the problems be solved. Yet, as time passes, it is likely that the profitability of children's shows will continue to increase, considerations of short-term financial consequences will become more important, and the difficulties of coming to grips with the problem will become even greater. Hence, the time and circumstances for formulating public policy on children's television would seem to be better now than they will be in the future.

POLICY OPTIONS

In approaching public policy on the children's television issues, the FCC could take a narrow view of its public-interest responsibilities and simply treat the issue of "potential harm" from advertising to children, or it could address the issue of the public-interest responsibility for affirmative standards for positive and constructive programming directed solely to the needs and interests of children. These issues, in turn, could be dealt with in one of three basic ways: (1) encouragement of self-regulation within the industry; (2) FCC imposed regulations within the existing industry structure; or (3) FCC policy directed to resolving the issues outside the existing industrial structure.

A long history of sad experience with self-regulation

indicates that this approach would simply amount to an exhortation to the industry to do better. Self-regulation is supposed to exist already over a broad range of broadcast-industry policies and practices. But all evidence indicates that it only works, if at all, for very short periods of time, when no significant financial interests are at stake. The NAB is supposed to be a focal point of self-regulatory power within the industry, but it functions very poorly in this respect, providing no compulsory membership, no membership accountability, and no effective sanctions. Twenty-five percent of the industry does not belong to NAB. No one knows what proportion of the industry abides by its recommendations because it has never been checked. The standards are not enforced. Perhaps the best example is children's television, which invariably turns into a veritable sea of ads during the Christmas season. Evidently, self-regulatory standards are only observed when there are no good reasons to violate them. Because of the substantial financial and profit interests in children's programming, self-regulation in that area is doomed to failure before it begins. An FCC decision to place hope for improvement on self-regulation would result in no appreciable change in existing practices or priorities. Perhaps a one-season, well-publicized flurry of activity might mark the zenith of the public-policy issue before practices reverted to the usual trend.

Alternatively, the Commission might choose to impose standards designed only to protect the child audience from the undesirable aspects of children's programming and advertising. However, these rules would prevent broadcasters from fully exploiting their profit potential, and because they would run directly counter to the economic interest of the firm, would therefore be subject to frequent violation. Moreover, it is doubtful whether the FCC could effectively police such standards.

In similar fashion, any FCC attempt to take affirmative action to enforce standards requiring a positive program of children's television directed toward the child's interests would also run directly counter to the economic interests of the broadcasters. It would also raise important problems of FCC oversight and control. The commercial, economic incentives would remain; the broadcasters and networks would be fully aware of all financial opportunities that were being denied them; and the basic determinants of children's programming decisions would still be advertiser market considerations. Although better than self-regulation, FCC-imposed standards are not likely to be able to come to grips with all aspects of the problem, or to be fully effective.

Finally, the Commission might remove children's television from the existing economic structure and incentives of the industry by disallowing all advertising directed toward selling products to children, i.e. all advertising except for institutional ads. This could prevent harm to child television audiences, but it might also prevent a sizable portion of children's television from being shown at all for lack of financial support. In like manner, a positive program for improvement of children's television would run into the same obstacle of devising a system of financial support to replace direct advertising revenues.

REMOVING CHILDREN'S TV FROM THE
COMMERCIAL MARKET

The external-financing option is the only alternative open to the Commission where it would not have to try to get the broadcasters to compromise, modify, or redirect their private pursuit of profit through sales of commercial advertising. Many analysts of the problem have concluded that it would be the most desirable alternative were it not for the accompanying financing problems, which could mean a loss of existing levels of children's programming.

There are two fundamental concerns about external financing: the first is, what the financial impact on the broadcasting industry from the loss in revenues would be; the second, what the sources of funds for program financing would be. In his recent study, FCC economist Alan Pearce looked briefly into these questions, concluding that within the existing structure of the industry, the revenue losses from children's programs would be substantial, and that institutional advertising and underwriting seemed to provide no ready supply of financial resources to assume the costs of supplying children's programs.

Financial Consequences

The financial impact of any major change on the existing broadcast industry depends largely on the time period over which that change would take place. In cases of instantaneous change, consequences may be enormous. On the other hand, over a time horizon of planned change, the consequences are not only much less severe but also, frequently, what was first feared as being detrimental to a firm may ultimately turn out to be beneficial. A considerable part of the fear of the consequences of change stems from the uncertainty of change relative to the stability of existing arrangements.

It must be emphasized that the Pearce model simply

made static revenue calculations, where the only change
was the quantity of revenue lost from the removal of
advertising from existing network children's television.
Moreover, the model assumed that the change to external financing would take place instantaneously, thereby
magnifying the consequence of the change upon network
profitability. Pearce recognized that if demand elasticity,
i.e. the response of advertisers to reduced supplies of
advertising minutes and possibly higher rates, was taken
into consideration, the revenue consequences would have
been much less severe.

Adverse profit consequences would be minimized even
further if all potential cost savings relating to promotion
and sales were considered. Approximately 30 percent of
broadcast expenditures are for promotion and sales
commissions. Most of these costs would disappear if
children's television were taken out of the commercial
market. Moreover, the networks have a unique capability to adjust their costs to changes in revenue in order to
maintain desired profit margins.[2] And when the economic consequences of the passage of time are considered
in the analysis, year-to-year revenue growth and the
opportunities for market adjustment become factors
easing the revenue, cost, and profit impacts of change.
Experience would indicate that the profit consequences
of removing advertising from children's television could
be substantially mitigated by market adjustments.

However, what is most important is that the acceptable level of financial impact can be used as a benchmark for determining the necessary time period over
which the change in financing methods can be phased in.
This is illustrated in Figure 5.

In Figure 5, point A represents total broadcast revenues for year *0*, the year before a shift to external

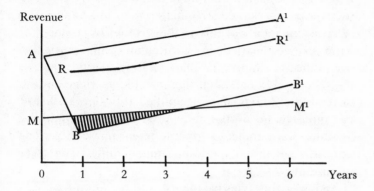

Figure 5. Phasing in Structural Change

financing would take place. The curve A–A^1 represents the anticipated trend in revenues under existing institutional arrangements for supplying children's television. The M–M^1 curve represents the minimum revenue level that the FCC decides the industry or individual firms must maintain to continue to operate at any predetermined level of financial health. If an instantaneous adjustment is made for the change to external financing, revenues would decline to point B, which is below the M curve. On the basis of the instantaneous comparison, it would appear that the change to external financing would be unfeasible and, therefore, an unacceptable alternative decision. However, if the change is implemented gradually over a period of several years, the annual impact in any one year is only a small fraction of its impact upon instantaneous adjustment. Thus, with a five-year phase-in period, actual revenues might become curve R–R^1 on Figure 5, substantially above the minimum acceptable revenues.

Whether a phase-in period of five years, three years, or eight years is adopted is immaterial to the basic issue. What is crucial about this analysis is that the number of years can be varied in accordance with particular circumstances. Moreover, the phasing period can be contracted or extended on the basis of experience in the early phases. And it could be applied at the level either of the industry or of the individual firm. It would be possible, for example, to apply different phase-in periods for different firms operating under different market circumstances.

Applying this type of analysis, the decision-maker is seldom faced with the confining alternative that the change to external financing cannot be accomplished because of economic reasons. If the decision-makers conclude that advertising to children should not be permitted on commercial television, they can adjust the economic consequences to the affected firms over time, by means of a phased strategy of implementation.

It must be recognized, of course, that the economic consequences of a change in the economic structure of children's television will affect more firms and industries than the broadcast networks and stations. Advertisers, agents, syndicators, and producers would also be affected. But here again, the process of adjustment to the new financing arrangements can reflect a sufficient time period for transition. Clearly, these entities do not have financial interests as great as the networks and stations; for virtually all firms the financial impact can be expected to be relatively modest, especially when it is recognized that most firms have acceptable alternatives, and in the course of development of the economy, will be adjusting to the changing opportunities and alternatives made available over time. The ACT proposal would simply take one profitable alternative away from them.

Although one could attempt to estimate the financial impact on each segment of the industry, the limitations of existing data and the infinite set of possible assumptions that could be pursued, would tend to make the precision of such forecasts an artificial focal point for debates on the children's television issue, when they should not be. There will always be differences in the assessments of the economic impact upon various affected institutions. When one recognizes that the FCC can develop a phased strategy for implementing change, monitor actual changes, and modify the rate of implementation of change as time passes if it so desires, precise forecasts of consequences become irrelevant to the fundamental children's television issues. Economic impact is a factor to be considered in designing a program for policy implementation. It is not a factor that limits the policy options available to the Commission.

Alternative Sources of Financing

Removing advertising from children's programming addresses the issue of protecting children from the harm of pinpoint advertising directed toward them. However, an affirmative policy of developing a minimum quantity and quality of children's programming intended to meet the needs and interests of children, requires consideration of the problem of alternative financing. This must come from such sources as institutional advertising, underwriting, or government. Here, too, to try to forecast the response of these institutions to the financial requirements of children's television is uncertain at best. The people directly involved, who would have responsibility for influencing such decisions, are hesitant to predict their reactions to the changed financial environment in children's television.

Whether or not external financing can be obtained for children's programming will remain a highly uncertain matter until it is tried. Institutional advertising is a widespread practice by United States corporations, but only a small proportion of their advertising budgets are devoted to it at present. In children's television, Health-Tex Inc., is the outstanding institutional advertiser, spending $1 million per year. Although the amounts of institutional advertising are gradually increasing over time, it is impossible to predict the potential response of institutional advertising to children's television opportunities under a changed system of financing. Potential institutional advertisers point out that they may well be interested, but their interest, and the amounts of their potential expenditure, will depend upon the particular circumstances, the program, the prestige, and other incentives that surround their support of quality children's programming. However, institutional advertising is more likely to support an established and on-going process of children's television than a new and developing one.

Underwriting support from foundations and other philanthropic grantors for children's programs is in much the same position as institutional advertising. Although the amount of program underwriting has been increasing in recent years, there is no reason to expect underwriters to assume responsibility for children's programming. However, it is reasonable to assume that underwriters would participate in the financing of children's television to a significant degree. The extent of their participation, though, is likely to be determined largely by the circumstances surrounding the new children's television operations. If it were prestigious and high-quality, and viewed as serving a public purpose, underwriting support could be fairly substantial. In contrast to institutional advertising, foundation support would be more likely to focus on the development and establishment of such a process, rather than the continuing operation of what already exists.

The United States Department of Health, Education, and Welfare (HEW) and other federal, state, and local government agencies spend substantial amounts of resources on children's educational films annually. To the extent that children's programs under the new arrangement can satisfy the requirements of these various agencies, as they should if they are directed to the needs of children, additional sources of financing could be uncovered. But here, too, one cannot forecast their potential participation with any degree of certainty because so much depends upon the nature of the children's television programming that might evolve under the new arrangements. Public children's television is being shown in schools at present. And any children's television that is designed and produced for the enrichment of children immediately overlaps the formal educational system, which spends substantial amounts of funds now on educational film and related activities.

It is clear, however, that the potential for attracting financing from institutions, underwriters, government, and other sources is there, if the new program structure is established properly and inordinate demands for funds are not made immediately. The practical problem is whether the funding potential can be tested without making an irrevocable decision to alter the structure of children's television.

By adopting the phasing procedure outlined here (Fig.

5) for providing the required near-term financial protection for broadcasters, a step plan can be devised to test the feasibility of phasing out advertiser financing of children's shows and phasing in external sources of financing. Although the phasing structure would be based upon a *long-run* plan, entailing complete conversion to external sources, the program could be established, at least initially, as an experimental one. The FCC could monitor developments, at least through the early stages, to see if sufficient funding was forthcoming from external sources. If it was not, the Commission could slow down the rate of changeover to the new structure with a minimum of inconvenience for all parties. Moreover, the Commission is always free to review its policy at any time.

This experimental approach has a unique advantage in that it gives those who have been requesting alternative sources of financing an opportunity to come up with the resources. If they do, the structure of children's television can be changed so as to respond directly to the interests of children. If they cannot obtain sufficient financing from external sources, alternative attempts to remedy the existing problems in children's television will have to be pursued.

A PLAN

The development of a plan for conversion to alternative financing arrangements for children's television must consider many interrelated factors. The annual rate of investment in children's programming depends upon the quantity of children's programs desired and the time period over which a library of quality children's programs is to be accumulated. The greater the quantity of new programs, and the shorter the time period over which they can be accumulated, the greater is the annual rate of investment required. Although one can set objectives for fund-raising to achieve a given program inventory level, the inventory of children's programs will grow at the rate that funding is attracted.

However, it is important to recognize that there is an existing inventory of quality children's programs. We are not starting from scratch. Moreover, as we have previously noted, children's television in particular does not become outdated easily, and the audience is continually changing as children grow older. Thus, the same characteristics that make children's television economical under existing economic conditions can make it economical under a system of alternative financing. For example, age-specific programming would be indefinitely valuable for periodic reruns. The fundamental difference would be that the programs, and their many reruns, would be designed for the needs and interests of children rather than of advertisers.

A first step in the implementation of an affirmative program for developing quality children's television would be an assessment of existing program materials and the classification of an inventory of acceptable programs. Such an assessment is required, not only as part of a plan to establish quality children's television, but also as part of one to protect children from the "harmful" characteristics of bad programming, such as violence. As earlier chapters point out, some of what is generally acknowledged to be the worst kind of programming is shown as children's television simply because its rerun costs are very cheap. As funding is attracted for the production of new children's programs, the established inventory of quality programs would increase.

Programming costs during the first several years under the new arrangements would be difficult to estimate because at least some development costs associated with the change in production arrangements would be involved. And even though the cost per showing may ultimately be lower than existing program costs, the financial resources for production are needed at the front end of the program cycle. As a point of reference, we know that existing commercial children's programs cost on the order of $125,000 per hour for program runs of about twenty individual half-hour segments. Children's Television Workshop (CTW) produced *The Electric Company* at a cost, including all background research and preparation, of approximately $8 million for its first 160 half-hour shows, or $100,000 per hour. *Sesame Street* costs approximately $5 million for 160 one-hour shows, or about $31,000 per hour.

If we use a liberal figure of $125,000 per hour as the upper extreme of what would be necessary for production in the first few years for program runs of about thirty hours per year, the annual program costs would run about $3.5–$4.0 million per hour of weekly children's television. However, if CTW's *Sesame Street* example is used as a more probable guide to costs, annual production costs would run only about $1 million per hour of weekly children's television. By establishing different trade-offs and assumptions about program costs, quantities, and other variables, a set of estimates can be calculated, ranging from approximately $1 million on up. This demonstrates that a program of alternative financing for children's television production clearly could be established with a threshold cost of a few million dollars to begin the first step in a phased program: the substitution of one hour of existing commercial children's programming with new, noncommercial, children's programming directed to the needs and interests of children. As more funds become available and additional programs are created, more hours can be substituted, until the ACT proposal of fourteen hours per week, or any other desired level and kinds of children's programming, is achieved. Once this state of maturity of program development is reached, financing requirements will diminish somewhat as new programming needs are limited to the continuing replenishment and reinvigoration of an existing level of satisfactory programs.

In the supply of children's television, there are other costs that must be incurred in addition to programming. These are essentially network coordination, television signal transmission, and broadcast station costs. Coordination of network distribution of noncommercial television is a function that could be very costly if it had to be especially performed for a few hours of children's programming. And it can readily be accomplished by the networks, as it is today, at minimum costs in their established system already devoted to continuous networking. In like manner, the costs of transmitting the television signal to broadcast stations would be minimized if the signals were delivered as part of the network's continuing broadcasting operations. Thus, performance of these functions could provide a contribution of the networks to the supply of children's programming under the new arrangements. The contribution of the broadcast stations would be the airtime over which the programs are broadcast.

Both broadcast stations and networks should be permitted, or encouraged, to contribute to the financing of programming. In fact, since children's television itself would no longer be a part of their public service responsibilities, financial contributions by stations might be encouraged or required by the FCC as a new part of their public-service responsibilities. However, programming decisions must not be made by stations, networks, or sponsoring financial contributors. An important part in implementing such a plan would be the development of a structure of separate decision-making entities to make programming decisions that reflect consideration of the needs and interests of children under the new decision structure, in which problems related to the basic commercial-system objectives, e.g. adjacent programs and advertising, do not color program production and selection decisions.

As a practical and feasible point-of-reference plan, a planning horizon of five to seven years could be adopted for the phasing out of advertising to children. Necessary lead times of six months to a year to establish a program under the new arrangements would be necessary. A four-to-eight-step procedure for transition would permit gradual and controllable change. In the first step, one or two hours a week of children's programming without advertising could be introduced—perhaps one hour of programming by each network for a national audience, and one hour of programming by local stations, drawing from both new programming and the existing inventory of acceptable quality children's television. Expansion of children's programming under the new arrangements could proceed as circumstances permit—primarily the rate of financing of new programs. This point-of-reference plan provides a manageable and reasonable transitional program. It can provide a foundation for the development of a more detailed, actual plan for implementation of the policy objective by the FCC, based upon its assessment of the more detailed circumstances of policy implementation.

In this last chapter we have developed a framework for examining the issue of children's television. The issue has been narrowed down to the purposes for which children are classified as special. As a special television audience, they need protection from pinpoint advertiser exploitation. In addition, they may require special programming directed to their needs and interests.

Under existing institutional arrangements for the supply of commercial children's television, the presently operative economic forces in the industry will tend to make today's problems in commercial children's television worse. Of the range of policy options available to the FCC, that of external financing has the greatest probability of success. A phased procedure along the lines of the point-of-reference plan described above appears readily manageable and feasible. The details of an actual plan for implementation are, of course, subject to debate and modification. What is most important, however, is that the plan be a complete one, designed to meet whatever objectives of children's programming are specified by the FCC as a matter of policy.

What we have outlined here is a method by which the FCC can design and implement such a policy without significant risk to the television industry or the public, and by which the FCC can oversee developments, modify policy over time if necessary, and control the rate of change. We now await a commitment to action from the FCC.

Notes

NOTES TO CHAPTER 1

1. Federal Communications Commission, "Notice of Inquiry and Notice of Proposed Rulemaking." Docket no. 19142, Jan. 20, 1971.
2. Address before the *International Radio and Television Society*, Sept. 14, 1971.

NOTES TO CHAPTER 2

1. FCC, "Broadcast Revenues, Expenses and Income of Television Networks and Stations, 1970–71" (Washington: FCC, 1972).
2. Several agencies have recently suggested that variable fee schedules would be more responsive to modern service patterns.
3. Sidney W. Head, *Broadcasting in America* (New York, 1972), p. 285.
4. Congressman Barry Goldwater, Jr., "Report on the United States Government and the American Radio-Television-Motion Picture Industry," August 1972.
5. Les Brown, *Television: The Business Behind the Box* (New York, 1971), p. 131.
6. Muriel Cantor, "The Role of the Producer in Choosing Children's Television Content," in C. A. Comstock and E. A. Rubinstein, eds., *Television and Social Behavior*, vol. I: *Content and Control* (Washington: Government Printing Office, 1971), p. 264.
7. See George Gerbner, "The Structure and Process of Television Program Content Regulation in the U.S.," in Comstock and Rubinstein, *Television and Social Behavior*, p. 408. Gerbner found that over 93% of all prime-time programming was reportedly under direct network control from conception to airtime.

NOTES TO CHAPTER 3

1. Maurice Shelby, Jr., "Children's Programming Trends on Network Television," *Journal of Broadcasting* 8 (1964): 247–54.
2. Les Brown, *Television: The Business Behind the Box* (New York, 1971), p. 65.

3. "Nostra Culpa," *Time*, Aug. 22, 1955, p. 47.

4. "Two Year Study by Communications Project on Viewing Habits of Children," *Newsweek*, April 26, 1954, p. 91.

5. "Before Their Eyes: The Show," *Television Age*, Jan. 8, 1962, p. 76.

6. Richard Schickel, *The Disney Version: The Life, Times, Art and Commerce of Walt Disney* (New York, 1968).

7. Shelby, "Children's Programming Trends."

8. Erik Barnouw, *A History of Broadcasting in the United States*, vol. 3: The Image Empire (New York, 1970), p. 65.

9. Irving Bernstein, *The Economics of Television Film Production and Distribution* (report to the Screen Actors Guild, Sherman Oaks, Calif., 1960).

10. Barnouw, *History of Broadcasting*, p. 110.

11. "Before Their Eyes: The Show," p. 7.

12. Neil Compton, "TV While the Sun Shines," *Commentary*, October 1966.

13. Barnouw, p. 150.

14. Arthur D. Little, Inc., *Television Program Production, Procurement, Distribution and Scheduling* (Cambridge, Mass., 1966).

15. "Minow Magic," *Newsweek*, Aug. 14, 1961, p. 66.

16. Neil Hickey, "What Is TV Doing to Them?" *TV Guide*, October 1969.

17. Melvin Helitzer and Carl Heyel, *The Youth Market; Its Dimensions, Influence and Opportunities for You* (New York, 1970).

18. Barnouw, p. 246.

19. "Always on Saturday and Occasionally on Sunday; Kids Don't Take Their Quarter Around the Corner to Loew's Like They Used to; Admen Are Learning," *Sponsor*, Jan. 23, 1967.

20. Barnouw, p. 207.

21. Brown, *Television*, p. 248.

22. Columbia Broadcasting System, Annual Report to Stockholders, 1963.

NOTES TO CHAPTER 4

1. Robert B. Choate, "The Selling of the Child," testimony before Consumer Subcommittee of the Committee on Commerce, United States Senate, Feb. 27, 1973, p. 5.

2. Helitzer and Heyel, *The Youth Market*, p. 218.

3. Ibid.

4. Ibid., pp. 181–82.

5. See John A. Howard and James Hulbert, *Advertising and the Public Interest*, a staff report to the FTC, March 31, 1973, especially chap. 6.
6. Helitzer and Heyel, pp. 196–97.
7. Ibid., p. 293.
8. Ibid., p. 216.
9. Norman S. Morris, *Television's Child* (Boston, 1971), pp. 56–57.
10. Muriel Cantor, "The Role of the Producer in Choosing Children's Television Content," in G. A. Comstock and E. A. Rubinstein, eds., *Television and Social Behavior*.
11. Ibid.
12. *Variety*, Sept. 15, 1971, p. 34.
13. Morris, *Television's Child*, pp. 180–81.
14. "Access Rule Increases Station Originations," *Television/Radio Age*, July 24, 1972.
15. "Kidvid '72: Quality Replacing Quantity," *Television/Radio Age*, Sept. 4, 1972, p. 61.
16. This was confirmed by the FCC inquiry into children's programming (Docket no. 19142). Of the stations filing responses, the independents presented an average of 22 hours and 40 minutes of children's programming per week compared to 11 hours and 36 minutes for the affiliates.
17. William D. Wells, "Communicating with Children," *Journal of Advertising Research*, as quoted in Robert B. Choate, "The Selling of the Child." Choate provides a detailed review of selling practices to children in this testimony.
18. Helitzer and Heyer, *The Youth Market*, pp. 32, 44, 50.

NOTES TO CHAPTER 5

1. George Gerbner, "Violence in Television Drama: Trends and Symbolic Functions," in Comstock and Rubinstein.
2. See also, Robert B. Choate, "The Selling of the Child."
3. The revised NAB Code standards that became effective Jan. 1, 1973 reduce the number of permissible commercial minutes in weekend daytime children's programs from sixteen to twelve per hour, and the number of interruptions from eight to four.
4. The FCC News Release announcing its Notice of Proposed Rulemaking and Notice of Inquiry on the ACT proposal is reproduced in the Appendix.

5. Ashbrook P. Bryant, "Television for Children, The FCC, The Public, and Broadcasters," in H. Skornia and J. Kitson, eds., *Problems and Controversies in Television and Radio* (Palo Alto, Calif., 1968).

6. Evelyn Sarson, "We As Parents Accuse You of the Five Deadly Sins," *New York Times*, Feb. 27, 1972, sect. 2, p. 17.

7. Bill Greeley, "Short 'Season' for Small Fry; Uplift Kidvid: Low on Originals," *Variety*, June 30, 1971, p. 41.

8. Jack Gould, "TV: Three New Formulas for Children's Programs," *New York Times*, Oct. 15, 1962, p. 59.

9. Alan Pearce, "The Economics of Network Children's Television Programming" (FCC, 1972).

10. Charles Winick, "Children's Television Commercials: A Content Analysis" (NAB, 1973).

Notes to Chapter 6

1. *Communications Act of 1934 and Amendments Thereto*, U.S. Government Printing Office.

2. See National Broadcasting Co. v. U.S., 319 U.S. 190 (1942); also, Red Lion Broadcasting Co. v. FCC 395 U.S. 367 (1969).

3. Ibid.

4. And, more recently, regulation of the emerging broadband (cable) communications technology.

5. "Red Lion Broadcasting Co. v. FCC," *Georgetown Law Journal* 56 (January 1968): 554.

6. See, for example, Nicholas Johnson, "Institutional Pressures and Response at the FCC: the Fairness Doctrine As a Case Study," in Gerbner, Melody, Gross, eds., *Communications Technology and Social Policy* (New York: Wiley, 1973).

7. Red Lion Broadcasting Co. v. FCC, 395 U.S. 367 (1969).

8. National Broadcasting Co. v. U.S., 319 U.S. 190 (1942).

9. Office of Communication of the United Church of Christ v. FCC, 359 F 2d 994 (1966) and 16 R.R. 2095 (1969).

10. Lee Loevinger, "Free Speech, Fairness, and Fiduciary Duty in Broadcasting," *Law and Contemporary Problems* 39: 286.

11. Roscoe Barrow, "The Equal Opportunities and Fairness Doctrines in Broadcasting," *University of Cincinnati Law Review* 37: 546.

12. 267 NYS 2d 415 (1966), per curiam 385 U.S. 12 (1966), rehearing denied, 385 U.S. 943 (1966).

13. 321 U.S. 158 (1944).
14. 321 U.S. at 167.
15. 1 Cal. Rptr. 665, 348 F 2d 98 (1959).
16. "Trespassing Children," *California Law Review* 47 (1959): 427, 429.

NOTES TO CHAPTER 7

1. FCC, "Notice of Inquiry and Notice of Proposed Rulemaking," Docket no. 19142, Jan. 20, 1971.
2. See, for example, R. Powers and J. Oppenheim, "Is TV Too Profitable?" *Columbia Journalism Review* (May/June, 1972), p. 10.

Bibliography

Articles

"ABC and NBC Alter Fall Kid Schedules," *Broadcasting*, March 10, 1969, p. 66A.

"ABC Comes on Strong as Children's TV Champion," *Broadcasting*, May 10, 1971, p. 19.

"ABC-TV Mapping After-School Special For Pre-Teen Set," *Variety*, September 15, 1971, p. 27.

"Access Rule Hurts Majors in Hollywood, FCC Analyst Tells Burch," *Broadcasting*, August 14, 1972, p. 40.

"Access Rule Increases Station Originations," *Television/Radio Age*, July 24, 1972.

"A little bit pregnant" (editorial), *Broadcasting*, March 27, 1972, p. 66.

"Always on Saturday and Occasionally on Sunday; Kids Don't Take Their Quarter Around the Corner to Loew's Like They Used to; Admen Are Learning," *Sponsor* 21 (January 23, 1967): 27–34.

"ANA Puts It in Writing On Children's Advertising," *Broadcasting*, July 10, 1972, pp. 23–24.

"Another Try For The Children's Eye," *Broadcasting*, November 29, 1971, pp. 69–70.

"As Kids' TV Gets More Learned, Networks Reap The Profits," *Television/Radio Age*, August 10, 1970.

"Aussie Animator Loses Round Vs. Hanna-Barbera," *Variety*, September 27, 1972, p. 28.

"Ban Against Advertising in Children's Programs?" *Broadcasting*, February 9, 1970, p. 56.

Barrow, Roscoe L. "Antitrust and the Regulated Industry: Promoting Competition in Broadcasting," *Duke Law Journal*, Spring 1964.

"Before Their Eyes: The Show," *Television Age*, January 8, 1962.

Bernstein, Henry R. "Broadcasters, Admen Hit Proposed Ban On Kids' Shows Commercials," *Advertising Age*, April 6, 1970, pp. 1, 81.

"Beyond Bugs Bunny," *Economist*, September 25, 1971, p. 54.

Blank, D. M. "The Quest For Quality and Diversity in Television Programming," *American Economic Review, Papers and Proceedings*, vol. 55 (May 1966).

"Broadcasters Fully Priced, TV Broadcasters' Prospects Mixed," *Standard and Poor's Industry Services: Current Analysis*, February 3, 1972.

Brown, Les. "Duffy and the Kidvid Code: Rival Webs Call It 'Showboating,'" *Variety*, December 15, 1971, pp. 27, 41.

———. "Kidvid's De-Klondike Blues: How Will Webs Recoup Losses?" *Variety*, February 2, 1972.

———. "The 'Enterprises' Behind Viacom," *Variety*, July 15, 1972, p. 32.

Brumbaugh, F. N. "What Effect Does TV Advertising Have on Children?" *Education Digest*, vol. 19 (April 1954).

Bryant, Ashbrook P. "Historical and Social Aspects of Concentration of Program Control in Television," *Law and Contemporary Problems* 34, no. 3 (Summer 1969): 610–35.

Burch, Dean. "The Chairman Speaks About Children's TV," *Television Quarterly*, vol. 9, no. 4 (May, 1970).

"Burch Suggests Webs Rotate Sked on Quality or Experimental Kidvid," *Variety*, September 23, 1970, p. 51.

"Children's Fare Stays Animated on Networks This Fall," *Broadcasting*, May 8, 1972, p. 52.

Christopher, Maurine. "Debate Over Definition of a Kid TV Show Stymies Reform Efforts," *Advertising Age*, February 7, 1972, p. 20.

Christopher, Maurine. "How to Finance Better Shows For Kids Is Pondered at ABC Session," *Advertising Age*, July 5, 1971, p. 31.

———. "Kids View Commercials Aplenty; CBS Runs Most, BAR Data Indicate," *Advertising Age*, March 1, 1971.

———. "3 Vitamin Makers Leave Children's TV," *Advertising Age*, July 24, 1972, pp. 2, 8.

Coase, Ronald H. "The Economics of Broadcasting and Public Policy," *American Economic Review* (May 1966).

Collins, Lawrence. "Sales Pitch to Wee One Mattel's Success Story," *The Boston Globe*, September 25, 1970.

"Commercial Time in Weekend Children's Programs Is Cut," *Code News*, National Association of Broadcasters, vol. 4, no. 11 (January 1972).

Compton, Neil. "TV While The Sun Shines," *Commentary*, October 1966.

"Costs Cited By Webs In Defense of Rerun Policies," *Variety*, September 20, 1972, p. 25.

"Costs of Non-network Fare Still Rising," *Broadcasting*, October 18, 1971, p. 76.

Cox, D. A. "Competition in and Among the Broadcasting, CATV, and Pay-TV Industries," *Antitrust Bulletin*, vol. 13 (Fall 1968).

Crandall, R. W. "Economic Effect of TV Network Program 'Owner-ship,' " *Journal of Law and Economics*, October 1, 1971.

Culhane, John. "Report Card on Sesame Street," *New York Times Magazine*, May 24, 1970, pp. 34–35.

———. "The Men Behind Dastardly and Muttley," *New York Times Magazine*, November 23, 1969.

Culkin, John M., ed. "New Directions in Children's Television," *Television Quarterly* 9, no. 3 (Summer 1970): 5–76.

Davis, Douglas. "The Underground Hours," *Newsweek*, October 13, 1969, pp. 105–06.

"Debating Advertising and Children's TV," *Broadcasting*, October 25, 1971.

"Disney's Five-Action Profile," *Business Week*, July 24, 1965.

"Don Taffner On International Kick With Kidvid To Fore," *Variety*, July 1971.

Eisner, Michael. "TV's Kidtime Entering Its 'Prime,' But Writers Are Key to Upgrading," *Variety*, September 15, 1971, p. 34.

Ferreti, Fred. "Children's TV Shifts To Fantasy and Quality," *New York Times Magazine*, March 5, 1970.

Fletcher, Alan D. "Advertisers' Use Of TV Ratings: Some Recent Changes, Implications," *Journalism Quarterly*, Summer 1971.

"Foreign Program Syndication: Why It May Be Threatened by the FCC Primetime Rule," *Television/Radio Age*, October 19, 1970, pp. 29–31, 55.

Forkan, J. P. "Advertisers Seek Image Benefits in Non-Commercial TV," *Advertising Age*, January 18, 1971.

———. "Did They Jump or Were They Pushed? Toy Makers Move Into Non-kiddie TV," *Advertising Age*, September 6, 1971.

———. "New NAB TV Code Rules for Toys Bring Woeful Industry Response," *Advertising Age*, February 1, 1971.

Fox, Sonny. "TV Versus Children," *Television Quarterly*, August 1, 1962.

Furman, Bess. "Parents Warn TV Over Child Shows," *New York Times*, March 30, 1960, p. 24.

Gardiner, Joan. "Playing the Game of Station Clearances," *Television* 25, no. 9 (September 1968): 26–29.

Gelman, Morris. "The Shows Stations Want: Are They in the Syndicators' Hats?" *Television*, vol. 25, no. 4 (April 1968).

Gerald, J. E. "Economic Research and The Mass Media," *Journalism Quarterly*, vol. 35 (Winter 1958).

Goldin, H. H. "Economic and Regulatory Problems in the Broadcast Field," *Land Economics*, August 1954.

Gould, Jack. "Agency Officials Tell FCC Who Is Responsible For What On Home Screens—It All Adds Up To a Primer on TV," *New York Times*, July 12, 1959.

———. "Fewer Pows and Sockos on a Saturday Morning," *New York Times*, September 8, 1969.

———. "TV: Three New Formulas for Children's Programs," *New York Times*, October 15, 1962, p. 59.

Greeley, Bill. "Dawn Not Coming Up Like Thunder on Saturday Kidvideo Anymore," *Variety*, September 15, 1971, p. 24.

———. "Kidvid Up to Old Tricks: Off and Running for the Ratings," *Variety*, September 13, 1972, pp. 39, 70.

———. "Short 'Season' For Small Fry; Uplift Kidvid: Low on Originals," *Variety*, June 30, 1971, pp. 41–48.

"Hanna-Barbera Earmarks $6,000,000 For Mixed TV Bag on Syndie," *Variety*, October 20, 1971, p. 37.

Harmon, L. "How To Pacify Parent and Educator Groups: Give Them Better Kids Programming," *Television/Radio Age*, March 20, 1972, p. 37.

———. "TV For Kids: Lotsa Answers But Always The Question—Who's Paying?" *Variety*, September 15, 1971, p. 63.

Heinemann, George. "Looking at Children's Television: A Self-Interview," *Television Quarterly*, vol. 9, no. 3 (Summer 1970).

Helitzer, Melvin. "Media Buying To Reach Children," *Media/Scope*, November 1963, pp. 61–65.

———. "No Second Chance in Kiddieland," *Sponsor*, July 20, 1964, p. 61.

———. "Youth—The Neglected $50 Billion Market, Part II," *Sponsor*, July 20, 1964.

Hickey, Neil, and Efron, Edith. "What Is TV Doing to Them?" *TV Guide* (October–November 1969), also in Barry G. Cole, ed., *Television: A Selection of Readings From TV Guide Magazine*, New York: The Free Press, 1970.

"Ideal's New Ploy In Network Buys," *Variety*, September 8, 1971.

"In Their Hands: Buying Power," *Television Age*, January 8, 1962.

"Into Their Minds: The Sell," *Television Age*, January 8, 1962.

"It's Open Season on Kidvideo: Confabs Bustin' Out All Over," *Variety*, September 23, 1970, p. 51.

Jones, Jack. "The Road To Improvement in Children's Programming," *Broadcasting*, October 5, 1970, p. 17.

Kahn, F. J. "Economic Injury and The Public Interest," *Federal Communications Bar Journal* 23 (1969): 182.

———. "Economic Regulation of Broadcasting as a Utility," *Journal of Broadcasting*, vol. 7 (Spring 1963).

"Kaiser String Debuts Kidvid Pubaff Project," *Variety*, September 17, 1972, p. 27.

Kaldor, N. "The Economic Aspects of Advertising," *Review of Economic Studies* (1950), pp. 1–27.

Kalven, H., Jr. "Broadcasting, Public Policy, and the First Amendment," *Journal of Law and Economics*, vol. 10 (October 1967).

Kelly, Katie, "The Junior Season Opens," *Time*, September 20, 1971.

Kennedy, R. "Programming Content and Quality," *Law and Contemporary Problems*, vol. 22 (Autumn 1957).

"Kiddie TV Ideas Offered," *Broadcasting*, December 21, 1970, pp. 9–10.

"Kids Programming Needs Surgery, Not Bandaid, ABC Affiliates Told," *Advertising Age*, May 17, 1971, p. 59.

"Kids TV Ads Mean $56,000,000 in Network Revenues," *Advertising Age*, July 24, 1972, p. 8.

Knight, Bob. "It's Put-Up Time in Kidvid: Will New Shows Mollify Critics?" *Variety*, September 8, 1971, pp. 31–47.

Knoll, Steve. "CBS Kidvid Plans Include Revival of 'You Are There,' Kid Newscasts, Mini Docus; Primetime News Specials," *Variety*, February 3, 1971, pp. 31, 50.

Kupferberg, Herbert. "Your Kids Need Better TV—You Can Help," *Parade Magazine*, January 30, 1972, pp. 20–21.

"Last Word On Children's Programming," *Broadcasting*, October 11, 1971, pp. 32–33.

Lee, R. E. "Inquiry Into Children's Programming—A Call for Action?" *Notre Dame Law* 47 (December 1971): 230.

Lees, F. A., and Yang, C. Y. "The Redistribution Effects of Television Advertising," *Economic Journal*, vol. 76 (June 1966).

Levin, H. J. "Broadcast Regulation and Intermedium Competition," *Virginia Law Review*, vol. 45 (November 1959).

Loevinger, L. "The Issues in Program Regulation," *Federal Communications Bar Journal*, vol. 20 (1966).

McDermott, John F. "The Violent Bugs Bunny *et al.*," *New York Times Magazine*, September 28, 1969.

McDonald, John. "Now The Bankers Come To Disney," *Fortune*, May 1966, p. 138.

McGowan, J. J. "Competition, Regulation and Performance in TV Broadcasting," *Washington University Law Quarterly*, Fall, 1967.

"Making A Move On Children's TV," *Broadcasting*, July 19, 1971, pp. 52–53.

Michie, Larry. "Kidvid Profits and Prospects: FCC Study May Lead To Changes," *Variety*, July 26, 1972, pp. 31, 43.

Minasian, Jora R. "Television Pricing and the Theory of Public Goods," *Journal of Law and Economics*, October 1964.

"Minow Magic," *Newsweek*, August 14, 1961, p. 66.

Morgenstern, Joseph. "Children's Hour," *Newsweek*, August 16, 1971, p. 9.

"Moves Toward Reform in Children's TV," *Broadcasting*, October 4, 1971, pp. 34–36.

Nathan, Gus. "Market Opening For Kid Programs," *Variety*, February 10, 1971, p. 34.

"NBC-TV Seeks More Tot Appeal," *Broadcasting*, January 19, 1970, p. 53.

"Next At FCC: Children And Commercials," *Broadcasting*, November 8, 1971, pp. 24–25.

"Nostra Culpa," *Time*, August 22, 1955, p. 47.

"No Support For Adless Kid Shows," *Broadcasting*, April 6, 1970, pp. 48–49.

O'Conner, John J. "Are They Doing Right By The Kids?" *New York Times*, September 26, 1971, sect. D, p. 19.

"Paradoxical Time In Children's TV," *Broadcasting*, September 13, 1971, pp. 15–18.

Peterman, John L. "The Structure of National Time Rates In The Television Broadcasting Industry," *Journal of Law and Economics*, 8 (October 1965): 77.

"Quieting The Children's Hour," *Time*, April 19, 1971, p. 75.

Ratner, Tom. " 'Freeze' Threat To Syndication Price Structure: Fleeting Spectre or Impending Reality?" *Television/Radio Age*, July 24, 1972.

Rothenberg, J. "Consumer Sovereignty And The Economics of TV Programming," *Studies In Public Communication*, Autumn, 1962.

"Round It Goes About Children's Shows," *Broadcasting*, June 28, 1971, p. 18–21.

Rustin, Dan. "Parents, FCC Making Networks Nervous On Kids' Programs," *Television/Radio Age*, November 30, 1970.

Sarson, Evelyn. "Growing Grass Roots in Viewerland," *Television Quarterly*, vol. 9, no. 3 (Summer 1970).

———. "We As Parents Accuse You Of The Five Deadly Sins," *New York Times*, February 27, 1972, sect. 2, pp. 17–18.

"Series Producers Continue To Gamble On Off-Network Syndication," *Facts, Figures and Film*, August 1971, p. 2.

Shayon, R. L. "Media Mystification," *Saturday Review*, October 17, 1970, p. 51.

———. "The Kidvid Ghetto," *Saturday Review*, June 20, 1970, p. 21.

Shelby, Maurice, Jr. "Children's Programming Trends On Network Television," *Journal of Broadcasting*, 8 (1964): 247–54.

"Something's Happening About Children's TV," *Broadcasting*, May 10, 1971, pp. 17–19.

Spencer, Walter Troy. "Television Production Costs Keep Going Up and Up," *Television*, 25, no. 9 (September 1968): 21–25.

Steiner, Peter O. "Monopoly and Competition in Television: Some Policy Issues," *The Manchester School*, May 1961.

———. "Programme Patterns and Preferences and the Workability of Competition in Radio Broadcasting," *Quarterly Journal of Economics* 66 (May 1952): 194–223.

"Talking Up To Children," *Time*, June 27, 1969, p. 68.

"The Children's Hour," *Newsweek*, December 22, 1969, p. 91.

"The Real Issue" (editorial), *Broadcasting*, March 13, 1972, p. 74.

"The Rush Continues On Children's TV," *Broadcasting*, August 2, 1971, p. 37.

"The TV Networks Shrug Off New Competition," *Business Week*, March 27, 1971, pp. 90–96.

"Threat To Program Development," *Broadcasting*, April 24, 1972, pp. 34–36.

"Tougher Than It Seems: The Kid Show Problem," *Sponsor*, August 6, 1962, pp. 29–50.

"Turmoil In The Program Market," *Broadcasting*, February 15, 1971.

"TV Production: Hands Across The Water," *Broadcasting*, July 31, 1972, pp. 39–40.

"TV Sales: A Record In The Making After Two Bleak Years," *Broadcasting*, August 21, 1972, pp. 14–20.

"TV's Saturday Goldmine," *Business Week*, August 2, 1969, pp. 96–98.

"TV Toy Advertising No Children's Game," *Sponsor*, March 11, 1963, pp. 28–30.

"Two-Year Study By Communications Project On Viewing Habits of Children," *Newsweek*, April 26, 1954, p. 91.

Vogl, A. J. "The Changing Face Of The Children's Market," *Sales Management* 93 (December 18, 1964): 35–36.

"What The Kiddies Prefer," *Variety*, February 10, 1971, p. 34.

Wren, Christopher S. "Magic Carpet That Transports? No, Dreamer, Not Yet. But We Do Have A Wall-to-Wall Drug Of Animation," *Saturday Review*, September 16, 1972, pp. 53–61.

"Young Animators Getting Scarce; Less Pix, Apathy," *Variety*, June 30, 1971, p. 24.

Books

Barnouw, Erik. *A History of Broadcasting in The United States*, vol. 3, *The Image Empire*. New York: Oxford University Press, 1970.

Bluem, A. William, and Squire, Jason E. *The Movie Business: American Film Industry Practice*. New York: Hastings House, 1972.

Broadcast Information Bureau, *TV Film Source Book*. New York: Broadcast Information Bureau, Annual.

Broadcast Information Bureau, *TV "Free" Film Source Book*. New York: Broadcast Information Bureau, Annual.

Brown, Les. *Television: The Business Behind The Box*. New York: Harcourt Brace Jovanovich, 1971.

Bryant, Ashbrook P. "Television For Children, The FCC, The Public, and Broadcasters." In H. Skornia and J. Kitson, eds., *Problems and Controversies in Television and Radio*. Palo Alto, Calif.: Pacific Books, 1968.

Cantor, Muriel G. *The Hollywood TV Producer*. New York: Basic Books, 1971.

Cherington, Paul W.; Hisch, Leon V.; and Brandwein, Robert, eds. *Television Station Ownership: A Case Study of Federal Agency Regulation*. New York: Hastings House, 1971.

Coleman, Howard W. *Case Studies in Broadcast Management*. New York: Hastings House, 1970.

Curran, Charles W. *The Handbook of TV and Film Technique: A Non-Technical Production Guide for Executives*. New York: Pellegrini Cudahy, 1953.

Dizard, Wilson P. *Television: A World View*. Syracuse, N.Y.: Syracuse University Press, 1966.

Field, R. D. *The Art of Walt Disney*. New York: Macmillan, 1942.

Garry, Ralph; Rainsberry, F. B.; and Winick, Charles. *For the Young Viewer: Television Programming for Children . . . at the Local Level*. New York: McGraw-Hill, 1962.

Halloran, J. D., and Elliot, P. R. C. *Television for Children and Young People*. Geneva: European Broadcasting Union, 1970.

Head, Sidney W. *Broadcasting in America*. Boston: Houghton Mifflin, 1972.

Helitzer, Melvin, and Heyel, Carl. *The Youth Market; Its Dimensions, Influence and Opportunities For You*. New York: Media Books, 1970.

Himmelweit, H.; Oppenheim, A.; and Vince, P. *Television and the Child*. New York: Oxford University Press, 1958.

Little, Arthur D., Inc. *Television Program Production, Procurement, Distribution and Scheduling*. Cambridge, Mass.: Arthur D. Little, Inc., 1966.

Madsen, Roy. *Animated Film Concepts, Methods, Uses*. New York: Interland Publishing Inc., 1969.

Minow, N. "Address to the Radio and Television Executives Society" (September 22, 1961). In L. Laurent, ed., *Equal Time: The Private Broadcast and The Public Interest*. New York: Atheneum, 1964.

Morris, Norman S. *Television's Child*. Boston: Little, Brown, 1971.

National Association of Radio and Television Broadcasters. *Television Station Management: Film Manual*, 1954.

Ogden, W. B. *The Television Business: Accounting Problems of a Growth Industry*. New York: Ronald Press, 1961.

Quaal, Ward L., and Martin, Leo. *Broadcast Management, Radio and Television*. New York: Hastings House, 1968.

Roe, Yale, ed. *Television Station Management: The Business of Broadcasting*. New York: Hastings House, 1964.

Sarson, Evelyn, ed. *Action for Children's Television: The First National Symposium on the Effect of Television Programming and Advertising on Children*. Chicago: Avon Books, 1971.

Schickel, Richard. *The Disney Version: The Life, Times, Art and Commerce of Walt Disney*. New York: Simon and Schuster, 1968.

Schiller, Herbert D. *Mass Communications and American Empire*. New York: Kelley, 1969.

Schramm, Wilbur; Lyle, J.; and Parker, F. B. *Television in the Lives of Our Children*. Stanford, Calif.: Stanford University Press, 1961.

Shayon, Robert Lewis. *Television and Our Children*. New York: Longmans, Green, 1951.

Steiner, Gary A. *The People Look at Television: A Study of Audience Attitudes*. New York: Knopf, 1963.

Television for Children. Foundation for Character Education. Boston: T. O. Metcalf, 1967.

Wells, William D. "Children as Consumers." In Joseph W. Newman, ed., *On Knowing the Consumer*, pp. 138–45. New York: John Wiley and Sons, 1966.

Other

Action For Children's Television. "Reply Statement in the Matter of Petition for Rule-Making Relating to Children's Television," submitted April 29, 1970.

"Comments," ACT. Filed with FCC, Docket no. 19142, Rm. 1569, July 2, 1971.

"Reply Comments—Action for Children's Television," October 1, 1971, filed with FCC, Docket no. 19142, Rm. 1569.

"Reply to Response of Romper Room to the Reply Comments of ACT," submitted to FCC, March 13, 1972.

Association for Childhood Education International. *Children And TV: Making The Most Of It*. Washington, D.C., 1954.

Baker, Robert K., and Ball, Sandra J. *Violence and The Media*, Staff Report to the National Commission on the Causes and Prevention of Violence. Washington, D.C.: U.S. Government Printing Office, November 1969.

Baldwin, Thomas F., and Lewis, Colby. "The Industry Looks at Itself." In G. A. Comstock and E. A. Rubinstein, eds., *Television and Social Behavior*, vol. 1. Washington, D.C.: U.S. Government Printing Office, 1971.

Barcus, Earle F. "Saturday Children's Television," A Report of TV Programming and Advertising on Boston Commercial Television, July 1971 (updated November 1971).

Bernstein, Irving. *The Economics of Television Film Production and Distribution*. Report to the Screen Actors Guild, Sherman Oaks, Calif., 1960.

Better Radio and Television. "Television for the Family, 1972 edition." National Association for Better Broadcasting, Winter, 1972.

Canadian Association of Broadcasters. *Broadcast Code For Advertising To Children*, October 1971. Revised, 1973.

Cantor, M. "The Role of the Producer in Choosing Children's Television Content." In G. A. Comstock and E. A. Rubinstein, eds., *Television and Social Behavior*, vol. 1, *Content and Control*. Washington D.C.: Government Printing Office, 1971.

Ducovny, Allen, Remarks before the ACT Symposium, October 18, 1971.

Federal Communications Commission. "Action for Children's Television Proposal Accepted as Rule Making Petition," Public Notice no. 44628, February 12, 1970.

Federal Communications Commission. "Amendment of Part 73 of the Commission's Rules and Regulations with Respect to Competition and Responsibility in Network Television Broadcasting" (Report and Order) no. 12782 (FCC, May 4, 1970).

Federal Communications Commission. Docket no. 19142, Station Responses and Other Filings.

Federal Communications Commission. "Interim Report By the Office of Network Study, Responsibility for Broadcast Matter" (1960).

Federal Communications Commission. Network Broadcasting House Report 1297, 85th Cong., 2d sess., 1958.

Federal Communications Commission. "Notice of Inquiry and Notice of Proposed Rule Making," Docket no. 19142, Federal Register 36, no. 20 (January 29, 1971): 1429–30.

Federal Communications Commission. "Report on Chain Broadcasting, 1941.

Federal Communications Commission. "Second Interim Report by the Office of Network Study, Television Network Program Procurement Part 1, 88th Cong., 1st sess., 1963, H. Rept. no. 281, p. 13.

Federal Communications Commission. "Second Interim Report by The Office of Network Study, Television Network Program Procurement Part 2, 1965.

Fleiss, David, and Ambrosino, Lillian. "An International Comparison of Children's Television Programming." Washington, D.C.: National Citizens Committee for Broadcasting, 1971.

Gerbner, George. "The Structure and Process of Television Program Content Regulation in the U.S." In G. A. Comstock and E. A. Rubinstein, *Television and Social Behavior*, vol. 1, *Content and Control*. Washington, D.C.: Government Printing Office, 1972.

Goldwater, Congressman Barry, Jr. "Report on The United States Government and The American Radio-Television-Motion Picture Industry," August 1972.

Liebert, Robert. "The Early Window: The Role Of Television In Childhood," American Psychological Association Convention, Washington, D.C., September 1971.

National Broadcasting Co. v. U.S., 319, U.S. 190 (1942).

Pearce, Alan. *The Economics of Network Children's Television Programming,* staff report submitted to Federal Communications Commission, July 1972.

————. *NBC News Division: A Study of the Costs, the Revenues, and the Benefits of Broadcast News*. Ph.D. dissertation, Indiana University, September 1971.

Red Lion Broadcasting Co. v. Federal Communications Commission, 395, U.S. 367, 390 (1969).

Roper Organization, "An extended view of public attitudes toward television and other mass media 1959–1971." Television Information Office, pp. 24–26. Section on "Commercials on Children's Programs."

U.S.A. v. NBC, CBS, ABC. "Antitrust Complaint," filed with U. S. District Court, Central District of California, April 14, 1972.

U.S., Congress, House, Committee on the Judiciary, Antitrust Subcommittee, *The Television Broadcasting Industry*, 85th Cong., 1st sess., 1957, H. Rept. 607.

U.S., Congress, Senate, Committee on Interstate and Foreign Commerce, *The Television Inquiry*, Report, 85th Cong., 1st sess., 1958.

U.S., Congress, Senate, Committee on Interstate and Foreign Commerce, *Television Inquiry, Part 4, Network Practices*, Hearings, 84th Cong., 2d sess., 1956.

U.S., Congress, Senate, Committee on Interstate and Foreign Commerce, *The Television Inquiry, The Problem of Television Service For Smaller Communities*, staff report, 85th Cong., 2d sess., 1958.

U.S., Congress, Senate, Committee on Interstate and Foreign Commerce, *The Television Inquiry, Television Network Practices*, Report, 85th Cong., 1st sess., 1957.

White House Conference on Children. Report to the President, Washington: Government Printing Office, 1970.

Additional Bibliography

Books

Land, Herman W. *The Children's Television Workshop: How and Why It Works* (Jericho, N.Y.: Nassau County Board of Cooperative Educational Services, 1972).

Articles

Choate, Robert B. "Fair Play for Young Viewers: How About Revealing Sponsor's Tactics?" *New York Times*, September 17, 1972.

Cooney, Joan G. "Isn't it Time We Put the Children First?" *New York Times*, December 3, 1972.

Johnson, Nicholas. "Institutional Pressures and Response at the FCC: The Fairness Doctrine as a Case Study," in Gerbner, Melody, Gross, eds., *Communications Technology and Social Policy* New York: Wiley, 1973).

Palmer, Edward L. "Formative Research in the Production of Television for Children," in Gerbner, Melody, Gross, eds., *Communications Technology and Social Policy.*

Robertson, Thomas S. "The Impact of Television Advertising on Children," *Wharton Quarterly*, Summer, 1972.

Ward, Scott, and Wackman, D. B. "Children's Purchasing Influence Attempts and Parental Yielding," *Journal of Marketing Research*, August 1972.

Other

Choate, Robert B. "The Selling of the Child." Statement before the Consumer Subcommittee of the Senate Commerce Committee, February 27, 1973.
————. Presentation to the NAB Television Code Review Board, May 26, 1971. Updated, October 1972.
————. "The Eleventh Commandment: Thou Shall Not Covet My Child's Purse." Statement before the Federal Trade Commission, November 10, 1971.

Howard, John A., and Hulbert, James. "Advertising and the Public Interest." Staff Report to the Federal Trade Commission, 1973.

Winick, Charles. "Children's Television Commercials: A Content Analysis," (NAB and Praeger Press, June 1973).

Appendix

Report no. 9621   January 21, 1971

CHILDREN'S PROGRAMS TO BE STUDIED BY FCC

A study inquiring into the amount and type of television programing available for children of various age groups, along with advertising content and methods of presentation, has been initiated by the FCC in a Notice of Inquiry and Notice of Proposed Rule Making (Docket 19142, RM-1569).

Pointing out that there are "high public interest considerations involved in the use of television, perhaps the most powerful communications medium ever devised, in relation to a large and important segment of the audience, the Nation's children," the Commission said it does not have sufficient data on children's TV programing upon which it can base a determination as to whether present use of the medium is reasonably satisfactory in relation to the high public considerations involved, and as to whether a substantial public interest question exists.

The action stems from a petition by Action for Children's Television (ACT) for rulemaking to set guidelines for all children's TV programs, including no sponsorship and no commercials, no use or mention of products, services or stores, or inclusion of brand names in any way. ACT requested that, as part of its public service requirement, each station be required to provide daily programing for children totaling not less than 14 hours each week, with programing for preschool children (ages 2–5) presented between the hours of 7 A.M. and 6 P.M. daily and on weekends; for primary children (ages 6–9), between 4 and 8 P.M. daily; 8 A.M. to 8 P.M. on weekends; elementary (ages 10–12), between 5 P.M. and 9 P.M. daily and 9 A.M. to 9 P.M. on weekends.

Statements in support of the ACT proposal generally supported better programing for children with less "hard sell" advertising. Statements in opposition urged chiefly that the ACT requests are violative of the First Amendment to the Constitution and the censorship prohibition of Section 326 of the Communications Act of 1934, as amended; that adoption of the proposals would contravene Commission policy charging licensees with the duty of making programing decisions that serve the public interest; that the proposal is unworkable because of the difficulty of definition and classification of programs for children, and that the prohibition of commercials is self-defeating since it will eliminate the major sources of children's programs because of funding problems. It was also claimed that the proposals would have an inhibiting effect on UHF television and other marginal stations, that the NAB has been and is capable of regulating the problem, and that the Commission should not substitute its judgment for parental control over programing for children.

The data which will be elicited in the proceeding is needed, the Commission said, for it to arrive at informed decisions. It emphasized that no conclusions have been reached and said that by Section 403 of the Communications Act, its authority to conduct the inquiry is not seriously open to challenge.

No final definition of "children's programs" is proposed for comment in the inquiry, but the matter of a suitable definition is among the general questions. For uniformity and reasonably accurate evaluation, general guidelines have been set out for use in presentation of material.

While programs chiefly involved are those primarily designed for children of preschool, primary, and elementary ages, stations and other parties are invited to list and comment on other programs of interest to children, even though the programs may not be primarily designed for them.

To provide guidelines, and to secure a representative sample of programs, the Commission has set up a composite week of Sunday, September 13; Monday, February 15; Tuesday, June 23; Wednesday, April 8, all 1970; Thursday, October 3, 1969; Friday, August 14, 1970; and Saturday, December 6, 1969, for use by station licensees and others in submitting factual information.

Noting that the listing of questions is not intended to limit the area of comment, the Commission requested data and comments as to the name, date, time, and length of programs designed primarily for children or of substantial interest to children, giving the age groups affected along with short descriptive program summaries. It seeks information as to whether the programs are entertainment or educational, original showings or reruns, and the program sources, as well as identification of the sponsors or advertisers; products, stores or services advertised and the commercial time involved. A definition of "children's programs" as used in each data compilation is also sought.

Other questions include suggestions for types of programs not now available; listing of benefits to children along with a definition of children's programing; and information on whether or not there should be restrictions (short of prohibition) on commercials, such as divorcement from program content.

While the proceeding is primarily one of inquiry, the Commission also labeled it a Notice of Proposed Rule Making, stating that possibly the data and comments supplied would provide a clear basis for a rule in some respects, and that it is desirable for the Commission to have maximum flexibility to take whatever further action the public interest requires.

Comments are invited by May 3, 1971; reply comments will be due June 1, 1971.

Action by the Commission January 20, 1971, by Notice of Inquiry and Notice of Proposed Rule Making. Commissioners Burch (Chairman), H. Rex Lee and Houser, with Commissioner Johnson concurring and issuing a statement, and Commissioners Bartley, Robert E. Lee, and Wells dissenting.

(Attachment omitted)

2. An NAB "Statement of Principles"

As part of its response to the FCC Notice of Inquiry and Proposed Rule Making, and the many criticisms leveled at children's television advertising, the NAB Television Code Authority in 1971 financed a content analysis of children's television commercials, excluding toy advertising, by Charles Winick. The study analyzed 236 television commercials directed toward children in September 1971. This represented all non-toy commercials shown during the month. The study examined the content parameters of children's television commercials as related to eleven criticisms of their specific content. Its results were to provide a basis for the establishment of NAB guidelines concerning children's advertising practices.

The long-awaited Winick study was released by the NAB in early June 1973, and was followed almost immediately by a "statement of principles" from the NAB Television Code Review Board:

STATEMENT OF PRINCIPLES on Children's Television Advertising adopted by NAB's Television Code Review Board, June 7, 1973. Applicable to Code subscribers and advertisers, it is to be effective no later than January 1, 1974.

Because of special considerations for children, the following principles shall apply to all advertising designed primarily for children:

1. Broadcasters believe that advertising of products or services normally used by children can serve to inform children not only of the attributes of the product/service but also of many aspects of the society and world in which they live.

2. Everyone involved in the creation, production and presentation of advertisements to children has a responsibility to assure that such material serves a positive function and avoids being exploitative of or inappropriate to a child's still developing cognitive abilities and sense of values.

3. Creative concepts, audio or video techniques and language addressed to children, shall be nonexploitative in manner, style and tone.

4. Documentation adequate to support the truthfulness and accuracy of all claims and representations contained in the audio or video of the advertisement must be made available to the broadcaster and/or Code Authority.

5. The disclosure of information on the characteristics and functional aspects of a product/service is strongly encouraged. This includes, where applicable, relevant ingredient and nutritional information. In order to reduce the possibility of misimpressions being created, all such information shall be presented in a straight-forward manner devoid of language or production techniques which may exaggerate or distort the characteristics or functions of the product.

6. Given the importance of sound health and nutritional practices, advertisements for edibles shall be in accord with the commonly accepted principles of good eating and seek to establish the proper role of the advertised product within the framework of a balanced regimen. Any representation of the relationship between

an edible and energy must be documented and accurately depicted.

7. Any representation of a child's concept of himself/herself or of his/her relationship to others must be constructively handled. When self-concept claims are employed, the role of the product/service in affecting such promised benefits as strength, growth, physical prowess and growing-up must accurately reflect documented evidence.

8. Appeals shall not be used which directly or by implication contend that if children have a product, they are better than their peers or lacking it will not be accepted by their peers.

9. Advertisements shall portray attitudes and practices consistent with generally recognized social values and customs.

10. Material shall not be used which can reasonably be expected to frighten children or provoke anxiety, nor shall material be used which contains a portrayal of or appeal to violent, dangerous or otherwise antisocial behavior.

11. Advertisements shall be consistent with generally recognized standards of safety.

In addition to the preceding principles, all advertising designed primarily for children is subject to review under the standards contained in the television code. The principles also supplement established television code guidelines, interpretations and policies that relate to various aspects of children's advertising.

The list of eleven principles read much like the Boy Scout Law advocating that television ads be creative, positive, responsible, nonexploitative, informative, truthful, documented, accurate, constructive, consistent, and reasonable. On the other hand, such ads should *not* be inappropriate, exploitative, misleading, exaggerative, improper, frightening, dangerous, or appeal to unsafe, violent, or antisocial behavior. Unfortunately, the statement of principles is nothing more than a string of gratuitous tautologies. There is really nothing unique about their application to children's advertising. The principles could readily be adopted for all television advertising. In fact, one would be hard put to find an advertiser, to either children or adults, who would not claim that he is presently fulfilling the statement of principles. It is interesting to observe that in issuing the statement, the NAB gave no indication that any existing advertising practices were in violation of the "principles," or that any specific changes in children's television advertising would have to take place.

The statement of principles deliberately avoids establishing any specific guidelines or standards on children's television advertising that would be enforceable in any way. Indeed, the major reasons for choosing an effective date of January 1974 appear to be: (1) to maintain an appearance of continuing self-regulatory action by the NAB while the FCC is deliberating its policy position on children's television; and (2) to avoid the sticky problem of explaining why the statement of principles would have no discernible effect on children's television advertising practices. Need we remind the NAB again that the new broadcast season begins in September? Or is the NAB holding out for an avalanche of children's advertising over the 1973 Christmas season that even the NAB can't accept as responsible, nonexploitative, truthful, and accurate? As an industry response to the stated concerns about children's television advertising practices, the statement of principles not only lacks substance but appears, in itself, to be a misleading and exaggerative advertisement.